G000279141

SEASONAL
SUICIDE NOTES

SEASONAL SUICIDE NOTES

My life as it is lived

ROGER LEWIS

CB

"*Seasonal Suicide Notes* is the funniest book of the year. This is comedy of a rare quality. Lewis is a seriously funny man."
Graham Ball, *The Sunday Express*

"*Seasonal Suicide Notes* is the most brilliantly funny and genuinely thought-provoking book of the year. Along with the lunatic jokes and napalm-coated insults, it is also a savage but cogent howl against contemporary culture. To the gas-filled balloon of today's literary world, puffed up to bursting with hype and spin, toadies and timeservers, networkers and overnight 'geniuses', Roger Lewis is a much needed prick."
Christopher Hart, *The Sunday Times*

"This is one of the strangest books you will ever read. It is also the funniest. And the most reckless... Buy the book, and be grateful you don't live next door." Byron Rogers, *The Spectator*

"If they ever award gold medals for comic genius, Roger Lewis will be a shoo-in for gold. This brief but hilarious memoir really should come with a health warning. Reading it may result in dislocation of the funny bone. If you like the taste of acid drops then give yourself a treat." Simon Griffith, *The Mail on Sunday*

"I cannot think of anyone I love or admire who would not enjoy receiving and reading this book. It's dark, savage, scabrous and enraged. A bilious hymn of hate against everything wrong with modern life, it is also the funniest, truest, most engaging thing I've read all year. Lewis is the drinking companion we all wish we had and reading this book you get the delicious sense that it's you and him against the world." Michael Gove, *The Times*

"Beautifully crafted... both funny and oddly cheering."
Roland White, *The Sunday Times* Comedy Book of the Year

"I suppose if you are not the target of Lewis's abuse, you may find it even more amusing than if you are, which is saying something. Simon Gray's diaries may have found a successor."
Philip Hensher, *The Spectator* Book of the Year

"These sulphorous annual round robin letters are not just crymakingly funny and profane: there are also arresting insights into art, literature and life. There are flashes of beautiful seriousness and the comedy is exquisitely well-observed."
Sinclair McKay, *The Daily Telegraph*

"A brilliantly splenetic diatribe... Lewis rages against everything. And an accomplished and funny job he makes of it, too."
Virginia Blackburn, *The Daily Express*

"You can't help but be sucked into the world of writer Roger Lewis. *Seasonal Suicide Notes* is, by turns, funny, tragic, tender and vicious... The combination of bile and self-knowledge is what gives it its comic edge." Stephen Moss, *The Guardian*

"Lewis is a five-star malcontent. His book is therefore killingly funny – the humour is the blackest, but it also finds room for a subtler, more wanly moving sense of the absurdity of life. Lewis knows what he is about as a writer."
Sam Leith, *The Daily Mail*

"Ironically, Roger Lewis's dyspeptic chronicle of a disenchanted soul is so sharply observant and deliriously funny that it makes you glad to be alive." Rupert Christiansen, *The Daily Telegraph*

"Hilariously angry... Hilariously rude... Yet here is the odd thing – there is something strangely cheering and life-affirming about it all." Terence Blacker, *The Independent*

This book was first published in 2009 by
Short Books
3A Exmouth House
Pine Street
EC1R 0JH

This paperback edition published in 2010 by
Short Books

10 9 8 7 6 5 4 3 2 1

Copyright ©
Roger Lewis 2009

Roger Lewis has asserted his right under the Copyright,
Designs and Patents Act 1988 to be identified as the
author of this work. All rights reserved. No part of this publication
may be reproduced, stored in a retrieval system or transmitted in any
form, or by any means (electronic, mechanical, or otherwise) without
the prior written permission of both the copyright owners
and the publisher.

A CIP catalogue record for this book
is available from the British Library.

Cover image © Alex Fox
ISBN 978-1-907595-00-4
Printed in Great Britain by CPI Bookmarque, Croydon

For

Gyles B., Duncan F., Steve M., and Francis W.
who laugh at my jokes

Previous Orchidaceae

Rewards and Fairies — *an edition*

Stage People — *a harlequinade*

The Memoirs and Confessions of a Justified Sinner
— *an introduction*

The Life and Death of Peter Sellers — *an elegy*

Charles Hawtrey: The Man Who Was Private Widdle — *a dirge*

Anthony Burgess — *a Cubist portrait*

Forthcoming

The Kill Fees Trilogy:
Growing Up With Comedians — *on clowns*
Ratbags and Sleazeballs — *on women and men*
Get a Life! — *on the art and science of biography*

Mister Jesus — *a gospel*

When I Was Young and Twenty and I Had a
Dainty Quim — *madrigals*

"Why should I not publish my diary? I have often seen reminiscences of people I have never even heard of, and I fail to see – because I do not happen to be a 'Somebody' – why my diary should not be interesting..."
The Diary of a Nobody, by George and Weedon Grossmith, London, 1892

"Did I have a serious side? Both sides of me are serious. It's pretty serious finding what's funny. You know when I was most serious? When I laughed at myself."
Mae West

The author and his father in their younger years

AUTHOR'S NOTE

WHO KILLED ROGER LEWIS?* Here's how it happened. After
the South Welsh upbringing, to which I frequently allude, I
went off to university, the first member of my family to cross
Chepstow Bridge and find a wider world. This remains my
only example of good timing. In any earlier or later eras,
when parents have been required to make financial contribu-
tions to a child's future, my education would simply not have
gone ahead. Not because my family was poor, you understand – but because money spent on me would have meant
less left for my father to spend on himself. When he went on
holiday, for example, he left me behind. I can't say I minded
in the least. I bear no grudge. I learnt to cook. I could watch
the television without noise and interruption. I loved the
company of Tog, our ancient Golden Retriever, and Emily,
the honking donkey, and I got my friends Nick Turner and

*How about *that* for what my hero Anthony Burgess called *an arresting
opening*?

13

Nick Prescott round and we drank my father's whisky cupboard dry. (Scotch he'd been given free by customers and farmers.) But the prevailing attitude remained – if I thought myself so high and mighty and unlikely to be fulfilled standing behind the counter of a butcher's shop, then what I had dinned into me was, "You made your bed. You lie in it." I had no encouragement, only cheap jeering. Or so I thought. I'm probably wrong. I was – and remain – too fearful and sensitive. Why can't I remember that I had my two-grand Blackwell's bill paid off? It was put through the accounts as combine harvester repairs. I still miss old Tog.

The only child in history whose role model was Uncle Quentin, the bad-tempered boffin from *The Famous Five*, I was an enormous success academically, because what other opportunities were going to come my way? (I wasn't so much of a success that I got frequently kidnapped, however – which was Uncle Quentin's fate.) But this – the First, the prizes, the Oxford junior fellowship* – never led on to anything really, perhaps because when I arrived, universities were starting to go off maverick intelligence and bright sparks, preferring instead bureaucrats and politicians and administrators, who'd take things like league tables and statistics seriously. Unfortunately, I go cold when given a form to fill in or sign. Rules and regulations give me the heebie-jeebies. Not for nothing had I early on made the decision

*Let us also not forget the challenge cup awarded to me as a Mixed Infant for being The Quietest Boy on the Bus, when we went on an excursion to Caerphilly Castle in 1969.

never to sit on a Committee or attend a Faculty Board Meeting. Other (still unbroken) vows included never in my life to set foot on a golf course or enter a McDonald's or KFC. But it was perfectly clear in the eighties doing English that if you possessed flash and dazzle, be a journalist.

It also didn't help that I was passionately interested in nutty actors, theatre, movies – subjects that a quarter-of-century ago weren't able to be studied at Oxford, where the syllabus stopped with Tennyson. Perhaps if Charles Hawtrey was a minor 17th-century figure instead of a mummer in the Carry Ons, I'd have been invited to Balliol to conduct my research, but it's too late now. Here and there polytechnics might have been starting up courses in media studies, but that wasn't going to be what I wanted to do either. I had a horror of impenetrable academic jargon, and I couldn't see why concision and liveliness were frowned upon – why writing badly and boringly was a path to permanent tenure and financial security. So I took the risk and went to France and wrote *The Life and Death of Peter Sellers*, giving it all I'd got; a headlong rococo text people are still coming to terms with, i.e, at 1,200 pages, possibly even now finishing. It did quite well – mainly because daughters bought it for their old dads, who'd laughed at *The Goon Show* and had heard of Harry Secombe. Few people saw that it wasn't a book about Peter Sellers – it was a book about a person *writing* a book about Peter Sellers. Laurence Sterne died in 1768 – exactly a century before the establishment of my father's slaughterhouse concern incidentally – and I wonder sometimes, crossly, swaggeringly and pompously, if in the meanwhile English literature has advanced a single inch.

If I missed the boat at university – they started to want to give jobs to people who knew about Structuralism and Semiotics, things I thought were simply frightful balls; and my simple pleasure in language, paint and performance for their own sakes was considered quaint and old-fashioned, a throwback to the days of David Cecil and John Bayley – then I next made the mistake, on returning from Normandy, of never living in London. If I was hiding away in the provinces, it was because I needed a big house for my money, which you'd think wouldn't be a controversial decision, or one worth penalising. With three children I was requiring the Gentleman's Residence in Herefordshire, not a bijou former artisan's cottage in Ealing or Wandsworth. But this has meant that I have never been part of the London literary clique. I am not an operator. I am part of no network. Sad mother Julie Myerson asked me only the other day, "Is writing what you do full-time? Sorry, I probably ought to know this." Arseholes to you, then.

Unlike Julie (b. 1960 in Nottingham, which must be as bad as Wales, but she now lives in Fulham) I have never been on *Newsnight Review*, or been asked to judge literary awards, or go to all the parties as a matter of course. When Mark Lawson had me on his radio show once, the expression on his blubbery face said, *who the fuck is this?* I met Rosie Boycott up the River Amazon – it was like she was being courteous and doing her best with a half-witted lowly heathen. Clive James said recently, "the literary world in London is quite small and everyone knows everyone." Small enough, I wonder, for me to kill them all off in ingenious ways, like the fruity actor played by Vincent Price in *Theatre of Blood*, exacting his revenge? James's is the sort of smug remark that makes me seethe. Yet had I hung about in town, for instance, or so I like to imagine, had I been less of a bee that swarmed alone, I'd have softened up the ground for the best thing I've ever done, my biography of my hero Anthony Burgess, which as a consequence never found a readership. Because it wasn't in the end actually a biography of Burgess, but a satire of the biographical form, full of Burgess's own grotesqueries and operatic or bombastic effects, with hundreds of mock-scholarly footnotes and elements of his Manchester music hall flamboyance. In truth, it did have one ideal reader – Professor Sir Christopher Ricks, whom I frequently meet at the circus, his son-in-law being Zippo, my son's boss. But domed-genius Professor Ricks resides in Boston, where he is editing *The Variorum Bob Dylan*. He has never heard of Mark Lawson, nor God bless him would he recognise Rosie Boycott if he ran her over.

On the whole, if as I do you live in the provinces, you've done a disappearing act – and the word provincial has connotations of mediocrity and the marginal and the third-rate, with small things becoming epically large: elderly choristers confessing before reporters and a photographer that half a century ago they joined the Cathedral Choir at the age of seven-years-and-eleven-months, instead of at the statutory

17

age of eight years; fire engines called out to rescue a hamster stuck down the sink; "timely warnings" from the vet about looking after your pigs during a heat wave – "Slurry levels should be lowered to minimise gas build-up and allow ventilation under the slats," readers of the *Hereford Times* were told... Evelyn Waugh might have officially lodged at Piers Court and Combe Florey, but if you look at his letters and diaries, for a hell of a lot of the working week he was at the Hyde Park Hotel and in the bar at White's. I'm seldom in the Groucho these days, particularly since funds ran out, so I am dismissed as a crank. Alexander Walker, who wrote a mediocre book on Peter Sellers that he pretended was authorised by the Estate, actually said as much once, sneering at me in the *Standard* for being the son of a Welsh butcher, and I don't mind admitting I was thrilled when the old poof died, I hope crushed by his bouffant hair-do. Why *should* I forgive such people?

What all this means one way and another is that there comes a point where you discover or wake up to the fact you haven't lately been living the life you expected or merited – a comic disjunction or delusion, as it happens, because of course we bring our own lives on ourselves, and I am fully aware that I am uningratiating and not tractable, that I seem to have a need to suffer, and that offered a welcome I run a mile. (I turned down membership of the Garrick, which hasn't happened to them before in its history.) I know that I am not capable of looking on the bright side of life, and cheerful camp-fire songs, kittens, puppies, doves, other people's beaming babies, Paris in the spring rain, country-side views and weddings make me irascible. Why can't I escape? Because people don't.

You think you're going to be Cary Grant. You'd settle for being Jeremy Irons. As my friend the late Willie Donaldson might have formulated it, you end up as Patrick Mower. Life wastes away, and yet this doesn't displease me. I actually now prefer my anonymous country life, shuffling between the remote Herefordshire Balkans and the dusty and forgotten Hapsburg spa-town of Bad Ischl in the Salzkammergut, where I spend half my year and can march around in my Wilhelmine way, meditating on the comic pathos of exile*. Where better to hide from the death of the West than in places where the clocks stopped a century ago? Bromyard, for example, is the last Ealing Comedy town left in existence, an island-within-an-island, where the continuity of Britain isn't a distant dream – where there are still cheerful green-grocers, butchers, bakers, a joinery workshop, and a champion little boozer called The Rose & Lion, where the Morris Men meet. There is a Norman church where the beauty of Evensong is preserved. There is a commercial hotel where you might dine on packet soup and waterlogged sprouts. The Town Crier is played by Stanley Holloway. I don't fit in with a world where the heroes are savage bullies, or should I say pantomime demons, such as Piers Morgan, Alastair Campbell,

---

*Not that Austria was technically (or loosely) ever historically Wilhelmine, but you catch my drift.

Gordon Ramsay* and Simon Cowell; where discussion of centuries' old literature and culture have disappeared from the landscape; where all the proprietors of newspapers and the heads of publishing houses want is stuff on DIY gardening and celebrity-shagging kitchen nightmares churned out by bloggers and wankers. You look through the brochures for literary festivals and their idea of a great writer is Ben Elton.

A seasoned old warhorse, whom I knew at Random House once and who is now at large in another conglomerate, said in an annoying faux-concerned and mock-sorrowful tone recently that it is such a shame good writing doesn't sell – but it is surely the *job* of these senior editors to ensure that it fucking *does*; it is infuriating when such otherwise smart people are part of the conspiracy to patronise the ordinary or general reader, to think that all they'll want or accept is shiny shite. "Oh I do miss John Grisham," I heard a publishing executive sigh, with what I interpreted as an insufficient amount of irony. I mean many of these editors went to Oxford and Cambridge. If it wasn't for the fact that Gyles Brandreth's rollicking Oscar Wilde-as-Sherlock Holmes novels are permitted to appear, I'd think it was all an utter betrayal of what they would have been taught once they'd got there. Everybody is in a state of complete surrender to the departments of finance and marketing, who

* Actually I won't have a word said against Gordon Ramsay, who pays out of his own pocket for five-year-olds with Spina Bifida to go to Zippos Circus.

reward the mediocre because that's the safest course. The country's best travel author, the heir to Bruce Chatwin; a theatrical biographer (who now takes in lodgers to make ends meet); a children's book illustrator (who is a part-time gamekeeper near Sandringham); and a once-upon-a-time Booker nominee (who is training to be a dog handler for the police cadets at Hendon) all tell me in high-pitched squeals or bass-notes of dread that, though they have recently delivered a new work, here's what typically gets said to them by way of a rejection: "It's a magnificent piece of writing, with not a splinter of chipboard in the whole rosewood sheen of it, really impressive, the Nobel Prize awaits, but this means nothing to the high street book-chains. Please accept *mes félicitations* – and regrets."

The high street book-chains say shit, publishers jump on the shovel. The girl at the till in the Hereford Waterstone's, by the way, once stopped me from autographing copies of my own masterpieces, because then "We can't send them back to the warehouse." I've never bought a book from the bastards since. I make my purchases on-line. I love the packages turning up. It is like Christmas.

Anyway – so much for English literature, of which traditional hardback publishers should be guardians. The passivity or lack of confidence is invidious and to me is a moral issue, as it has the same effect in the long term as Mao's breaking ballerinas' legs and spitefully putting intellectuals in the paddy fields during the Cultural Revolution.

Their excuse no doubt would be to say, as was said to me

recently, admittedly by an American, "We are powerless to make oiks read what they don't wish to read." But I'm an oik. I'm from industrial South Wales, where my great-great-grandfather George Gardner Lewis sold pigs' dicks to the miners for their dogs*. My oik pedigree is impeccable and goes back to the days of Twm Shon Catti, the cave-dwelling Welsh highwayman and illegitimate son of Sion ap Dafydd ap Madog ap Hywel Morthen of Pont-y-Ffynnon, Cardiganshire, though I don't suppose they call it Cardiganshire now. But I had great teachers every step of the way – at Bedwas Mixed Infants, Machen Juniors and Bassaleg Comprehensive; then later at St. Andrews and Oxford. There was the Bible at Sunday School, Bunyan and Robert Louis Stevenson in Mrs Harrington's class, Dickens and Homer (in translation) by the age of ten. I still have my well-thumbed copies. I know farmers in Raglan and out-of-

---

*Cousin Jeremy's great-grandfather. Jeremy Lewis is my more successful alter-ego, a Fellow of the Royal Society of Literature, on the committee of this and that, generally much-loved. He sometimes even appears as a coach on writing courses in Puglia, sponsored by *The Oldie*. I've threatened to enrol as a pupil, to see if I can find out at last *just how it is done*.

Here's a funny thing. I was once at a grand dinner at Magdalen College, Oxford. An old buffer said to me, "You wrote a wonderful book on Cyril Connolly!" "No, that was my cousin." "Ah yes, of course. Tobias Smollett! Marvellous!" "Sorry – my cousin again." So it went on through Jeremy's complete works. In the end I had to say, "Okay, so you've rumbled me after all! I can't fool you any longer, silly old buffer that you are. Yes I'm he. Tell me, what did you *really* think of *Grub Street Irregular*?" On the whole I find it is generally easier to be other people than it is to be myself – no wonder I wrote the definitive biography of Peter Sellers.

work port-wine salesmen in Cwmbran who can still quote yards of *As You Like It*.

At no point, however, were any of us prepared back then, in the sixties and seventies of the last century, for a world with Simon Cowell in it, a man whose eyes gleam like Count Dracula's, and who has a genius for promoting artists who are simultaneously trash and tremendous popular hits – a man who is only interested in being successful commercially. "It is fine being artistic," he told a blind piano-player on *American Idol*, "just not on this show" – a show for which Cowell receives in excess of $33 million a season. On *Desert Island Discs* in 2006, Cowell's book was *Hollywood Wives* by Jackie Collins and his luxury a mirror*. According to a profile in the *Sunday Times* by Ariel Leve, he "shuns intellectual elitism" (e.g. Proust, Bergman films, *coq au vin*) and admires Victoria Beckham for admitting she doesn't finish books, because "it's better than lying. Why lie about it?"**

And Cowell or Piers Morgan or Alan Sugar are looked up to as role models, and they are endemic. It is a mystery to me why publishers and editors, people who in their guts must want to oppose them and the philistinism they represent, are so *weak*. (Uncle Quentin wouldn't have lasted five minutes on *The Apprentice*, even allowing for the fact he'd have been kidnapped in the lift on the way up.) They should fight this

---

* On the offchance that they ever get me on, my book is *Five on Kirrin Island Again* by Enid Blyton and my luxury a loaded revolver.
** Cowell earns full marks, however, for supporting The Association of Children's Hospices, a national charity.

war, not cave in. I don't believe they can't do anything about it, that it's nothing to do with them – and Waterstone's and Amazon and the credit crunch seem to me an excuse for their *own* latent philistinism – even sadism; one senses a sanctimonious pleasure is being had when they ditch anything erudite. There's a quiet relief around the office, as they free themselves of the bother and the burden of promoting an inspired genius in favour of shifting further coffee-table tributes to Jade Goody. A world in which my show-off hero Anthony Burgess could make so much from his cryptic books and rambunctious literary journalism, which took in subjects as various as James Joyce and Beethoven, Shakespeare and Malaya, and which incorporated such an admittedly daft vocabulary – *acroamatical*, *aleatory*, *allophone*, *apocope* – that he had to live in tax exile, has rapidly disappeared. I know from personal experience that sub-editors today will delete any vaguely esoteric reference or big word. And Burgess died only in 1993 – not 1893 or 1793.

Of course I am not unaware of the fact or irony that had I myself been born in the eighteenth century, or cast as the original of Sir Nathaniel, the curate in *Love's Labour's Lost*, I'd still be the one complaining and in a state of torment because, for example, Latin and Greek was on the way out and nobody was buying my pamphlets on Marcus Fabius Quintilianus. As Max Beerbohm reminds us, "Gladstone used to quote whole strings of Latin hexameters, mostly from the *Aeneid*, in his parliamentary speeches, and the

House understood him. Already one discerns a debasement of English, and other debasements will follow that." Indubitably so – but, though Cicero and Virgil may have been lost, Max and Gladstone didn't know about the two fat cooks dressed in fishermen's-knit cardigans, Zoe Ball's *Live and Kicking*, Jeremy Spake, the camp Russian-speaking baggage-handler on *Airport*, or full-of-beans ex-drug addict Davina tracing her ancestry, in *Who Do You Think You Are?*

There are some of us who are always going to be born in their wrong era – in exile in time as well as space, unsettled and still as it were pulling our wagon across the frontier – but at least my pioneering fatherhood days are definitely well in the past. What this means today is that my lot has grown up and might (who knows?) eventually leave; but a lot of people my own age are only now getting around to having toddlers and worrying about schools – and I suppose they don't want to face this, but when wee Candida and Clamydia and Ptolemy and Rohypnol are in their twenties, the dads will be under the sod and their mums in Marrakesh with a new husband met on Friends Reunited. I can't generate much sympathy. Another reason why perhaps I did not gravitate Londonwards and why I'm like Ovid on the Black Sea is that I was married at the age of twenty-two, soon spawned three children, and developed different and larger priorities, not to mention acquired different, more immutable responsibilities – and as likely as not by not raising them to be dumbed-out and grasping, in introducing them (when I had the where-withal) to crumbling opera houses, zoos, circuses, gloomy out-of-season hotels and picnics on steam trains, I quite failed them? (They are clueless about money.) We never went to Euro Disney or a sports event; we didn't have up-to-date computers or go to Centreparcs. I poured wine down their throats from an early age and they had to put up with my fuddy-duddiness and refusal to do anything I personally found boring (an extensive catalogue).

Whilst I was the worn-out young parent in a falling-down French farmhouse fifteen years ago and the rest of my generation was networking like billy-o and ensuring I'd never catch up, it was infuriating to receive every Christmas a pile of ghastly boastful round-robin letters, in which people went on about their marvellous lives. And it is happening again or still happening. If I was sceptical about the happiness tidings and gleeful seasonal dispatches years ago, and was envious, quite frankly, that my life wasn't nearly as nice as everyone else's, then as surely as cats piss up walls I can't believe any of it today – not a sausage rings true, if I might mix a metaphor.* People seem to me to be simply delusional. Yet we now receive round-robins from middle-aged persons who are newly proud parents and who will go on about fancy foreign holidays, pony club triumphs, examination attainments, and the like, and I'm enraged because I know from my own long experience that real life isn't like this in the least. Mostly, families mean horror and despair and worry,

* Ringing sausages? Bejaysus and be-feckun-gorrah! I must hie myself to a writing course in Puglia.

more like the Munsters as conceived by Strindberg than the Simpsons and mushy Waltons.

This book, therefore, is my own personal bulletin from the frontline of a twenty-first century existence, where at the rainbow's end there is no pot of gold. It is a Francis Bacon scream on behalf of every pudding-faced person who has been generally disrespected, passed over at work, who is in thrall to his own ungrateful, feckless children, who is starved of affection, short of money and recognition, feels like a Third-Worlder, and who when looking at glossy adverts in magazines or on the Tube, with all those photographs of lovely bodies, doesn't find these commercials *aspirational* – they are a ferocious *rebuke*; they emanate from a world from which you'll be forever barred, if only because your belly is so big it hides your shrunken willy or (girls) your tits are so saggy you step on them in the shower. Come on, admit it. Let's stop pretending. Invitations to orgies at the *Playboy* Mansion have dwindled, haven't they? Your fingers and palms have broken out in weeping eczema or psoriasis and you are covered in unravelling soiled bandages from the *stress* and the sheer endless critical *frustration*. This is a book for the many millions of good people for whom nothing has gone according to plan and who are, as Peter Finch says in *Network*, before he kills himself in full view of the television audience, *mad as hell*.

2004

January

MY FATHER HAS DIED, getting the year off to a more than usually bad start. Cancer of the bumhole, one of God's prime custard pies. He'd been ill and fatally deteriorating for two years, so this wasn't unexpected news, let's face it – but ever since his death I've been as moody and morose as Hamlet, particularly as being the eldest son my sole inheritance is to comprise of spare bumper packs of Coloplast Direct Wetwipes and Coloplast Direct Water Spray, for use in the vicinity of the Colostomy Bag. I've got a few of those too, for when my turn comes. Not quite in the same class as disappointingly losing the throne of Denmark, I grant you. But *still*.

Back last November he wasn't expected to last the night. We rushed to the Heath Hospital in Cardiff – he was bloated (chronic fluid retention from kidney failure) and covered with blood-red rashes (from the septicaemia), and resembled a sea monster – the one Marcello Mastroianni and Anouk Aimée gaze upon in the last scene of *La Dolce Vita*. He then went to a hospice in Penarth, where not unexpectedly but nevertheless off-puttingly, people kept dropping dead around him — multi-cultural families would be weeping and wailing without embarrassment, renting their garments, the business. Believe me, there's no touching or any shows of affection where my clan is concerned. The Lewises' sensitive hearts are proudly armoured against feeling, and I myself was never taken onto anyone's lap as a child and held.

He went home for Christmas, where the dining room was turned into a bedroom. The downstairs phone is in the dining room and Mrs Troll* lost no time in starting to get competitive prices and quotes from funeral directors. If hearing is the last faculty to go, my father will have been inadvertently eavesdropping on all this haggling. My niece Della went in and strummed her harp — a nice gesture but again a confusing one for a man already well on his way up the stairway to Heaven.

He looked strangely youthful as he faded away, sleeping more and more, forgetting to want to eat, slipping into a coma. The thing is — he always looked like this, an effigy of a Grail Knight on his tomb. My main memory of my father is of him flat out and sleeping on the sofa throughout the day. People would come to dinner (as luncheon was called) — he'd slink off and fall asleep, often if they were

*Our beloved, temperamental housekeeper — like Mary Poppins or Nanny McPhee as envisaged by the Brothers Grimm. She may well have been ultimately Scottish, like Nanny Dolly, my grandfather's wet nurse who lived out her retirement in a hut attached to the slaughterhouse.

in the middle of talking to him. Tosca the Cavalier King Charles Spaniel used to curl up and snooze on his belly. Bolder visitors would try and make light of this, and take photographs. Ronald Reagan's speechwriter Steve Masty who'd flown specially to South Wales from Egypt for the weekend was outright indignant.

I can see now that he was bored and depressed beyond endurance, unhappy and unfulfilled, stuck having to be a farmer and a butcher, his wicked bully of a father having refused point blank to allow him to carry on at school. I think this is why he had mixed feelings about my own career – he was in a foul mood during my graduation ceremony. He only came to see me at Magdalen if a lift could be cadged from Auntie Marion and Uncle Eifion, Arwyn and Margaret Rees or Geoffrey Morgan, Welsh neighbours for whom I'd be expected to push the boat out. The education he'd craved, I'd had. By getting a degree, I was leaving him behind – so I was always to be gently mocked, until I was the one who seemed pitiful. My wanting to rise above my circumstances was both a rejection and a criticism. He'd rather it had been him, in my place. I didn't appreciate or properly discern his mirth and curiosity until much later.

I grew up being treated as a namby-pamby creature who never did a stroke of getting-your-hands-dirty real work, laughed at in a nasty sort of way, as if I was an aesthete who walked around wearing a beret. For years though I went every Saturday with old Jack Francis in the van around Caerphilly and along Pandy Road delivering meat. Sundays were spent sorting out the sheep ready for the slaughtering on Monday. The summers I spent hauling hay bales and straw bales. I was unable to make a secret of the fact I found agricultural labour a soul-killing and futile cycle of drought, and storms, and bad crops.

What an obnoxious, ungrateful child I must have been in my parents' eyes, moody and psychologically displaced (and the child is father to the man, let me get that in before a root-faced reviewer does so) – a freak of nature, compared with everybody else in South Wales, where it steadily rained soot. Though I had all I ever wanted and demanded, from books and puppet theatres to a Super-8 cine camera and Emily the donkey, I was convinced that any minute an emissary on a galloping horse from the Royal House of Bourbon would turn up and reveal that owing to an error or plot with switched babies at the font in St. Barrwg's Church, I was in reality a Crown Prince or heir to the Grand Duke of Calabria or something similarly Ruritanian. I craved decorum.

But the message never came. Instead we lived in unheated premises above the butcher's shop. When I played my Igor Stravinsky records or LPs of *The Goon Show*, the hammering and chopping on the block below made the stylus needle jump and lurch across the vinyl, adding to the discord, augmenting the violent forces. The carpets were covered with sawdust and Mrs Troll was always charging around with the Ewbank, swinging it from side to side, possibly even above her head as if she were a competitor in the annual Braemar Highland Games, denting the wainscot, chipping the paint, the tubes and pipes of the primitive, wheezing vacuum cleaner covered with sticking plaster and soiled bandages. Any boldness and fun in that poor woman's personality had long since been replaced by a cantankerous and unpredictably explosive temper. She took to wearing trousers, the elasticated waist hitched up under her armpits. I have emulated every particle of her nervous vehement energy.

Though as a female presence she was as comforting as wire wool, a trait she got from her Peebles mother, an unsmiling flinty party who'd been an interrogator during the war – the Franco-Prussian War of 1870 in all probability, where she'd have been on the same side as Count Otto Von Bismarck, helping hands-on-hips virago-fashion to organise an invincible army, beating back the French from the Rhine and annexing Schleswig-Holstein by force of her personality – fair play to Mrs Troll, she was proud of the whiteness of her wash. She used to iron my father's handkerchiefs and leave his clothes immaculately laid out on the bed every day. If he was going out in the evening, there would be his Cirencester tie, his golden cummerband and tasselled Masonic apron.

A near life-size drawing of Mrs Troll and Pinget

Mrs Troll's mother used to

visit us on occasion and go off on little day trips on her own by dragon-red Western Welsh coach to places like Glastonbury or Bath Abbey. She collected souvenir hunting horns. When she died, older than Methuselah, Mrs Troll found thousands of the fuckers. I have one or two by my bed to this day – it is a running joke that when I give a toot for somebody to come and bring me coffee or adjust my pillow I will be ignored. If I was the Grand Duke of Calabria I wouldn't be treated this way.

~

The undertakers came and took away the body at three in the morning. I assume my father *was* dead and there was no more jumping the gun. That would have been mean. The atmosphere here is weird and surreal, bright and brittle, feverish, sickish. People keep offering to make me sponge cakes, which is what the Welsh do at a time of crisis. There's a tragedy, they get cracking with their Magimix.

The undertaker has asked us if we want to put mementoes in the coffin – so we have gathered together my father's Russian religious icons, a Billie Holiday CD, an XL Brecon Jazz Festival 1997 t-shirt, some marzipan, sea shells from Barfleur, a decanter of whisky, plus other bric-a-brac. Everything is going in – a pharaoh's lumber for the afterlife? No, it's more like a skip. Archaeologists in future centuries will be scratching their heads. The corpse has been dressed in a blazer with brass buttons, a Savile Row cravat, pink shirt and patent-leather dancing pumps. He must be off to meet his maker looking like a thirties adulterer, lacking only an ebony cigarette holder. Steve said "On his cloud I hope he roared with laughter to see himself decked out as Maurice Chevalier, God bless him."

Anna and I went along to the churchyard – the plot was laid out and marked with a wooden stick. *Mathias Lewis* was written on it in felt pen. When I went along again later, two cheerful chaps were digging the grave and listening to a radio, like a scene out of a modern production of *Hamlet*. The soil was red and thick – I remembered how it used to cover my father's wellies. It is an idyllic spot, with views over the fields – a gate, a wooden stile, a mossy path. Though soon before we'd had the year's shortest days, it felt already like midsummer, pungent and soporific.

The undertaker Mr Joyboy (as I wished he was called) was there in person, a big-boned matter-of-fact chap, like the Fat Controller in the *Thomas the Tank Engine* stories. I found it rather pleasant, witnessing the practicalities, the men lifting out stones and boulders and the hole getting to be about ten feet deep, so there'll be room eventually for me, my mother, Emily the donkey, old Tog, even our beloved three-foot tall housekeeper Mrs Troll, should the Grim Reaper ever pluck up the courage and dare get near enough to wield his scythe.

~

Llandaff Cathedral was packed with over five hundred mourners. My mother, a breeder of Welsh Mountain Ponies and an NSPCC fundraiser, and from whom I normally like to keep a safe distance, preferably of approximately several hundred miles (we don't get on), was resplendent in the front pew in bible-black bombazine. Benign but distant, she's always preferred animals to people – as who doesn't deep down, Her Majesty The Queen included? Mrs Troll sat next to me – though she is so short, when she stood up to sing, people thought she was still sitting down. Indeed, that she was crouching on the floor. I wonder, though, of all those farmers, butchers and Rotarians who also turned up, crooked of limb and growling and yapping, was my father able to talk to a single one of them about what interested him most – books, plays, opera, art, foreign films? How many other South Welsh butchers subscribed to the *New Yorker*, the *Times Literary Supplement*, the *London Review of Books* and *Granta*? He'd leave behind the old copies in the waiting room at Velindre Cancer Centre, Whitchurch, where he had the chemotherapy. In his French house he watched Louis Malle's *Vanya on 42nd Street* so often the tape wore thin. He told me he particularly appreciated Sonya's final speech – perhaps the most revealing thing about himself he ever said to me:

> *We shall live through a long succession of days and endless evenings. We shall bear patiently the trials fate has in store for us... When our time comes we shall die without complaining. In the world beyond the grave we shall say that we wept and suffered, that our lot was harsh and bitter... Yet we shall rejoice and look back on our present misfortunes with feelings of tenderness, with a smile...*

Anyone identifying so deeply with Chekhov has had a

life that gave no satisfaction. My father had inherited the shops and the slaughterhouse and the farming enterprise that had been going since 1868 and succeeded only in seeing it all fizzle and get eaten up with bank overdrafts. I wonder now if he did this deliberately – an act of belated revenge upon his inflexible father, who'd controlled his spending and who'd generally squashed him, exposing him to a world of hurt and suspicion. On the two or three times we went to Tenby, he had to return to the shop in time for the weekend trade. He was begrudged a minute off. His brother and business partner, my Uncle David, was so distressed at the parlous finances, when he and Auntie Janet eventually found out, the two men had a fight with meat hooks that was the talk of Newport Market for weeks. Had not the slaughtermen Ron Curnow and Jack Francis intervened, it would have been murder.

They sold up in 1994. Apart from sleeping more than ever, my father peeled buckets and buckets of spuds for Mrs Troll's stew cauldron. She did the Iona to Mull pilgrim walk, but still didn't manage to lose herself off the edge of a rugged glen in the fog – a missed opportunity on the Almighty's part I felt.

~

He was not an obtrusive man – he finally shook my hand on the morning of the day I was married. I remember no other physical contact. His most intense delight was hunting for mushrooms. He'd rise early and set off with a wicker basket across the fields and past his flocks and herds – only to be met, as likely as not, by a neighbour walking in the opposite direction, *his* basket fully laden. "Morning, Mathias!" he'd say brazenly, without breaking his stride. My father would then turn back for home.

~

After the funeral service we drove in procession to the churchyard in Caerhays. We had to have Cousin Looby with us, as she was too fat and awkward and wheezing with asthma to fit into anyone else's vehicle. We followed the coffin to the grave, where it was expertly hoisted with straps straight into the hole. The vicar recited the Nunc Dimitis. I deem it a small triumph that I'd persuaded The Rev. Jeremy to find a copy of The Book of Common Prayer and do a proper service. He'd looked genuinely surprised. "Most people want excerpts from *The Lion King*," he said.

Everybody was weeping – except me. I caught sight of Looby tottering perilously on a slope in the distance, unable to go forwards or backwards, and I had to have a good laugh. In her younger days Cousin Looby had danced with Michael Heseltine at a Conservative Fundraiser in Swansea. She'd not manage the foxtrot now.

At my mother's request, Mrs Troll had made posies from the garden for the womenfolk to toss into the grave. I was expected to approach Mr Joyboy and be given a pinch of builder's sand, which I cast into the pit, catching my first (and only) sight of the coffin without its flag and other adornments. It seemed to have fancy brasswork on the edges of the lid, elaborate screws at the corners. No wonder it cost

£2995 + VAT and had to be delivered by train from Derby.
In a semi-circle, behind the mourners, stood half-a-dozen of
Mr Joyboy's assistants, as formally dressed as minstrels,
with their white gloves and top hats. Mr Joyboy gave a low,
theatrical bow to the grave, and it was over. As we returned
to the car, the young gravedigger was arriving with an arm-
ful of spades. "I'm off to fill him in for you now !" he said
with a huge smile, a fellow of infinite jest.

~

My mother had booked a room at the Courcey Hotel for
brown sherry and a choice of sandwiches. This was the first
time in history Mrs Troll had ever been seen in an outfit
other than her floral-patterned tabard pinafore. The place
was packed with familiar faces, uncles and aunties and
Rotarians and yokels and yeomen, Welsh people with low-
slung hairy bottoms. Uncle Eifion and Auntie Marion made
a beeline for the eldest son and heir (me) to express their
condolences in emotional voices – they seemed in quite a
rush, perhaps needing to get back home and revise their
Christmas card list as we have none of us ever heard from
them since. I'd spent the day wearing my father's Gieves &
Hawkes suit, which retained his smell and here and there a
strand of his hair. I found this enormously consolatory.
People aren't dead if you don't want them to be. We'll be
joining them in oblivion soon enough.

February
I decided to spend a month in a hut in the Canadian Rockies

built by a Red Indian. Feeling I was as a fountain sealed with its own ice, I thought I'd find the deserts of snow a solace. I love the severe cold – the bleakness of the mountains in the blue distance – the wolves and bears and ghosts. Actually, after three days I got bored and found myself watching a slide show in a museum devoted to ammonites.

March
Nothing happened.

April
To Rome for an audience with Pope John Paul II, *in re* a future project of mine, *Mister Jesus*. I can see the posters already – "The Book You've Waited Two Thousand Years For !" There'll be an Anglican fatwa issued – I'll be attacked in the street by little old jam-making ladies and crucifix-wielding boxing nuns, "Jab, Sister, jab !"

What a pagan city this is, with all the ancient ruins scattered about and chaps dressed as gladiators lurking by the Colosseum. The Pope looks mummified, as if he's died and they haven't told him yet. Anna's father had his wallet pinched on the subway, so we wasted a morning can-celling his credit cards and filling in forms at numerous police stations. I was then due to go to New York for the *Ring* cycle at the Met, but backed out because I was too depressed to leave my bed. My Anthony Burgess book is published in America by St. Martin's Press. They didn't seem very excited by my offer to go over and publicise it.

Indeed – the reverse. Some of the reviews are homicidal.

May

A few days in London. Lunch at The Ivy with Mark Booth, my esteemed editor from Century; champagne at the Garrick all afternoon; an *Oldie* Luncheon at Simpson's in the Strand for Francis Wheen. I used to absolutely adore a week like that. Anyone would think that I'd made it – so why do I feel more insecure and anxious than ever?

Saw the film of my book *The Life and Death of Peter Sellers* at the Curzon Mayfair – my name literally up in lights. Went with Barry Cryer. Geoffrey Rush wearily and perfunctorily said, "Oh, Roger, hi!" to me in the bar before whizzing off at top speed as far away as possible. Indeed, he hopped in a taxi and went to Australia.

It takes all my willpower to stop myself from grabbing these mimes by the neck and spelling it out ever so succinctly that "Without my *fucking* book you wouldn't have had a *fucking* film, let alone one which is winning you all these *fucking* awards !"* I'm in enough of a temper anyway – because the film was in the Sélection Officielle at the Cannes Festival the other day and I wasn't invited because, as the horrible publicity woman Fishface Wetwipe** said, I was "only the author." I threatened to fly myself to

---

* For his outstanding performance in *The Life and Death of Peter Sellers*, Geoffrey Rush won the Emmy, the Golden Globe, and the Screen Actors' Guild Award, amongst other plaudits.
** Not her real name.

the Côte d'Azur and march along the Croisette with a sandwich-board saying, "This is my film and they won't let me in!"

The production company's Big Cheese got wind of my scheme and called me from his mobile in an extremely irate fashion, as the sympathetic newspaper coverage I was getting looked as if it might scupper his little coup – for Charlize Theron to walk along the red carpet arm in arm with Britt Ekland. "Who put sand up *your* vagina?" I wanted to say to him queenily.

With every cause to hate it, I can report that I admired the film enormously – an enjoyable pastiche of a Sixties romp, but a supermarket pop video version of the biography, which is an altogether madder and stranger and stronger portrait of the sad genius. Barry and other friends thought it was a total mess, narratively incoherent and preten-

"Moi, Peter Sellers" poster

tiously edited. Stephen Hopkins' visual style seemed much indebted to Peter Lydon's Arena documentary, *The Peter Sellers Story As He Filmed It*, which had made ingenious use of home movie footage. Miriam Margoyles who plays Peg (Sellers' doting mother) without changing her costume or make up could go on to play Mrs Troll without strain. Indeed, without changing her costume or make up, Miriam could play *me* without strain.

June

Stayed up in the bar until dawn at the Groucho drinking Brandy Alexanders with a drunken MP. Wish I could remember who he was.

July

Made a documentary for Sky Italia, called *Profondo Rosa – La Vera Storia della Pantera Rosa*. I refused to leave home to be interviewed, so a film crew came here to the Herefordshire Balkans and set up their kit in the Ptarmigan Hotel, much inconveniencing the landlady. Indeed, the landlady and Mine Host kept criss-crossing in the background, fiddling with light switches and generally muttering. I think they did this on purpose. It would have been funny if by the end they were putting on straw boaters and feather boas and high-kicking it across the bar, hoping against hope to be noticed. I was paid in cash (euros) from a plastic bag.

~

Went to a Buckingham Palace garden party with Anna.

Behind us in the queue going in were quacking and nervously giggling Midlanders, several as I understand it invited for their "services to the funeral industry in Wolverhampton." We were there under Anna's auspices. It was like a musical sequence designed by Cecil Beaton, the frocks and hats and morning coats. Two tents were set up at opposite ends of the lawn, each containing a military brass band. When one band finished playing, a flag was hoisted to signal to the other lot that they could start on their medley of songs from the shows. Here and there I noticed dried poo in the grass – corgi shit! Only the prospect of a furious black look from Prince Philip stopped me from popping it into a Buck House serviette and auctioning it that night on ebay. I could have retired on the proceeds.

August

A few days at a hotel in Tenby that should call itself Guest House Paradiso. The bathroom window covered with bird droppings. The dining room panelled with fixtures and fittings rescued from a steam ship. Gloriously shabby and atmospheric and deserted – exactly my kind of place. I have since learned that it has burned down.

~

Then to the Lake District – a place never before visited by me. Our hotel was once a house rented by Beatrix Potter. I liked the brass and mahogany pleasure steamers on Lake Windermere. A pilgrimage to Brantwood, on Coniston

Water, home of John Ruskin. I much identify with Ruskin, sitting in his turret scowling at the owls. At one time I thought I'd be a contemporary Ruskin, doing for nutty actors what he did for modern painters or Venice's stones. I'd have settled for being Bernard Levin. I've ended up a disconsolate literatus, clipping out funny stories from the *Hereford Times* for a toilet book.

~

Tristan meantime was in Taizé, France – some massive God Squad operation, where they sit round singing "Kumbaya" and it is expressly forbidden to be found smoking drugs. The atmosphere is so tranquil, one of the monks got stabbed.

September
Went on the wagon for five days, but nearly died of boredom. Oscar, my second son, who spends a fortune texting the friends he's just spent all day with, decided he wanted to switch schools – from the excellent Bishop of Hereford Bluecoat School to a place in Tenbury Wells I've never heard of. We said yes, so long as he sorted it all out himself. Which he did. Content in or with my own South Welsh Comprehensive, I've never once wanted to waste money on the children's education that might be better spent on myself, i.e., being a 365-bottle-a-year man, on drink.

~

Sébastien, meanwhile, started at The Chantry High School, Martley, Worcestershire. He's growing up at last and stopping thinking he's a Hobbit, who has to have special Hobbit meals on Hobbit plates served on a Hobbit tray in his Hobbit bedroom, with its Hobbit eiderdown and Hobbit curtains. Once he discovers girls the Tolkien merchandise will be in the St. Michael's Day Hospice Charity Shop faster than *winking*. I said winking. Stop making up your own jokes.

October

The Life and Death of Peter Sellers is released nationwide to lukewarm and shall we say mixed reviews (many truly terrible) and a pathetic box office revenue. Will I ever receive my percentage of the producer's take?* Paul Bailey said apart from the cleaners he had the cinema to himself when he went along in the afternoon, "And poor Miriam looks absolutely ghastly!" The make-up department did indeed go to town, especially in the funeral parlour scene, where a be-rouged Miriam lies in an open coffin. Paul once met her in person and as large as life at a finger buffet.

November

Did a gig at the Cardiff Screen Festival, the Welsh for screen as was pointed out numerous times in the bi-lingual brochure being *sgrin*. It follows therefore that the cinema in Islington will have to be *Sgrin on the Grin*, should a Welsh

* No. (2009)

The foaming Toby Jug of an author with Peter Lydon (peeping) and Joe McGrath (left)

person need directions to it. Joe McGrath and Peter Lydon also present*. Huge fun — we discussed how Sellers needed to live a life of total sensation and excitement, or else he collapsed into fits of bored depression and despair — hence the cars, cameras, gadgets, girls. Everything a distraction. When

---

* Joe McGrath directed and put up with Peter Sellers many times — *The Magic Christian*, *The Great McGonagall*, a series of advertisements for Barclays bank, as well as *Casino Royale* — about which a whole book should be written, capturing the Age of Aquarius indulgent mood. Peter Lydon masterminded the definitive three-part *Arena* documentary, *The Peter Sellers Story — As He Filmed It*. In more recent times he has directed that Billie Piper series where she's a ho, *The Secret Diary of a Call Girl*. Boys, am I really alone in looking at bang-tidy Billie's mouth and cheeks and thinking, *Jesus H. Corbett*! *She could get your balls in*!

Joe worked with him in *Casino Royale*, he had the impossible task of arbitrating between the warring egos of Sellers and Orson Welles. There were five people in our audience, one of those being Joe's wife.

December

Saw our beloved housekeeper Mrs Troll for the first time since my father was put under the sod. We screamed at each other with loathing after twenty minutes. The gallons of bad blood that's cascading can't be quantified. All because I poked fun at her floral-patterned tabard pinafore. She'd been to see about her slice of the Will and said in a true witch's cackle, "I'm off to *Florida*, Rog. I'm off to *Florida!*" She was snarling and euphoric – triumphant. Oh well, good for her if she has a few shillings. My mother has her Welsh Mountain Ponies to keep her happy and is off to follow in the footsteps of Freya Stark, her pen pal. I've been effectively barred from Mrs Troll's retirement home next to the slaughterhouse – so have never seen the new kitchen cabinets, the new conservatory extension, the new carpets and curtains and wallpaper throughout. I have not seen her new Welsh dresser hung with colourful mugs or Pinget the dog she got given by the hospice nurse – though I heard that when Pinget pissed up her new curtains she booted him to kingdom come. I'd like to think that it was Mrs Troll who pissed up the curtains and *Pinget* who booted *her* to kingdom come, but life's never fair.

2005

ANOTHER SPIRIT-CRUSHING year. Criminally underpaid and under-employed, laughed at by editors if ever I ask for a few of Craig Brown's stray crumbs; derided by the critics, who instead of treating me like my hero Anthony Burgess say I am more like Guy Burgess, exiled if not in Moscow then in the Herefordshire Balkans, where I stand in the street poppy-eyed and waving a knobbled stick; betrayed by friends, one of whom turned round after twenty years of accepting my hospitality with alacrity and said that the Peter Sellers story was after all his own personal copyright (I put the police onto him for fraud – the lesson is: never trust a man with a nylon hair transplant – I thought he was cultivating London Pride on his head); *disrespected* and *over-looked* and *humiliated* – the usual stuff. No wonder my book on Jesus will be another Method Biography. As Milligan said, whilst waving a gun at his own head, "Christ had it easy !"

January
Tristan's eighteenth birthday. We decided to hold a black-tie

party at Whitbourne Hall. Unfortunately a few guests went to Whitbourne Village Hall by mistake, where the locals were putting on *Cinderella*. A chap who'd driven all the way in the sleet from Oswestry sat through the first act thinking Tristan was Buttons. The evening began in a civilized fashion, with the youngsters rather beautifully turned out. A hundred eighteen-year-olds and a free bar are not a good combination, however. Before long they were getting emotional in the toilets, throwing up everywhere and generally behaving like those chimpanzees at Bristol Zoo who wore nappies and fought over a teapot. The Gentlemen of Jive, the live band I'd hired, was over-amplified and able to be heard over seven counties. A Group Captain who arrived in full mess kit and medals was mistaken for the ex-doorman at the BBC's Aeolian Hall. Duncan Fallowell and the Queen Mother's former favourite flower-arranger at Clarence House signally failed to get on. Aunty Pawsey refused to attend because her invitation had arrived later than Aunty Majolica's invitation. None of Tristan's Welsh family managed to turn up, despite having had plenty of warning. Eighteen years, to be precise. It was also one year ago exactly since my father died.

February
A no-frills flight with Anna from Coventry aerodrome to Venice and the Do Pozzi Hotel. Sébastien was conceived in Room 23, now a shrine. Infertile couples make pilgrimages and leave with beatific smiles on their faces. I am making a

study of the bits of bone and Holy Foreskins found in Venice's reliquaries, for the *Mister Jesus* book, or as it is now called, *The Sexual History of Christ*. My theory and one no more fanciful than Dan Brown's is that if you piece together the Holy Foreskins you'll get a set of matching luggage.

March

To Paris and a hotel recommended by Duncan Fallowell. Amazingly it was not filled with musclemen spray-painted gold but was rather elegant and next to a glove shop. Went to the Picasso and Francis Bacon exhibition at the Musée National Picasso in the rue de Thorigny. What a useless painter Bacon was – all those smeary faces and placenta pinks. He had one idea in his life: paint people (Popes particularly, or Dan Farson) as if they are inside out and being buggered. His pictures on display next to Picasso's only emphasized his amateurishness. The slaughterhouse screams are adolescent. Bacon had no idea how to paint shoes, wristwatches or hands. Nobody has been capable of competent draughtsmanship in England since the death of Augustus John.

~

On to Barfleur, Normandy, where Tristan and his girlfriend Hannah-Susannah had spent all day preparing an elaborate dinner – hard-boiled eggs and a bit of spaghetti.

~

Invited to give a lecture at the University of Central

England, Birmingham – an institution of learning hitherto unknown to me situated under a motorway flyover in an area exclusively populated by multi-cultural persons in national costume. Mosques, supermarkets with yams and kumquats piled on the pavements, shops with metal grilles on the windows, a cinema that is now a carpet wholesaler. Rather surreal that in this environment there are earnest academics toiling at scholarly editions of Sir Walter Scott's *The Heart of Midlothian*.

April

Nobody else bothering to be available, not even the caterers or chaps in charge of the mobile toilets or honey wagons, in desperation Warner Bros. had to ask the pissing *author* to publicise the DVD of *The Life and Death of Peter Sellers*. As I didn't want to go to London, I spent hours and hours in a cupboard at BBC Radio Worcester, talking to invisible interviewers down the microphone. This did give rise however to the year's highlight – my spot on *The Bernie Clifton Show*. The chat went very well, despite there being the alarming sound of a hurricane coming from Bernie's end. Was this an outside broadcast and was Bernie manfully hosting his show from the end of a pier (in Sheffield?) whilst wearing his amusing chicken costume? Being stuck in my cupboard, I can shed no light on this mystery. Anyway, the DVD got much nicer reviews than the original film. I particularly like the deleted scenes.

~

As I'd reviewed her memoirs very favourably, Lauren Bacall invited me to her party at the Ivy. Didn't go because I preferred to stay at home watching *Footballers' Wives*. Amber discovers that Pundarik was covered in fake tan when he died, meaning that Tanya has her baby. Meanwhile, Shannon checks out Harley's story and Noah dates the beautiful Bethany.

May

Oscar is released from having been grounded since Tristan's party, where he led the field in the puking and bottle smashing antics. My children are sometimes a terrible disappointment. They've never even been fairly competent on the recorder. Spent much of the month in bed with depression – I hate the spring. A photograph of me in *The Malvern Gazette* makes me look like a shoplifter in Budgen's – doughy, yellowish, porcine, and furtive.

June

Anna and Tristan commence their injections for Tanzania, a place I have no intention of ever visiting. You don't need malaria tablets for Tenby.

~

Missed the Faber party because (a) there'd be too many people there I'd cheerfully like to stab in the eye with a fork and (b) *The Bill* was on. Zain Nadir searches for a missing fourteen-year-old whose online romance has led her into danger, and a guilt-stricken Gabriel reveals to Sheelagh that he deliberately killed the Sun Hill sniper by pushing him from a rooftop.

July

To the Salzkammergut. I love the faded spa town of Bad Ischl, where the Emperor Franz-Josef spent his summers in a mustard-yellow villa. There are parks and gardens with fountains and wrought-iron bandstands, fin-de-siecle pastry shops and concert halls. The café at the railway station has chandeliers and a worn marble floor. The thermal baths are hushed and spooky – white-clad nurses pad about. Hitchcock heroines could be abducted here and kept under unwilling sedation.

~

What an off-putting language German is, though. It's all *Faht*, *Fuchs* and *Kunst*. I am not a competent linguist. Trying to search for a word-compound that meant "Is this house near traffic?" (*Verkehrsanbindung*), what I came out with was "Haben Si mit der Frau Verkehr gehabt?" Or, "Did you have intercourse with this woman?" The expression of pure gibbering shock on the estate agent's face was a marvel. His hair went grey. He must have thought I was from the Secret Police, and all was known.

~

As it will be our Silver Wedding Anniversary on July 31st 2007, I said we should now send Aunty Pawsey her invitation.

August

Their systems crammed with £400 worth of rabies jabs and yellow fever injections apiece, Anna and Tristan are in Tanzania. That's Tanganyika to me – the former colony of German East Africa mandated to the British in 1919 under the Treaty of Versailles. Unlike Bob Geldof, I can't get worked up about Africa. As regards food shortages, you try getting a fresh lemon in the Co-op on a Sunday night and all that matters is an emergency gin and tonic. Anyway, in giving my donation to Live8 I just asked for the Swiss bank account numbers of the African prime ministers. This'll save on the postage. Until governor-generals and district commissioners played by Terry-Thomas and Ian Carmichael are reintroduced, complete with their ostrich-plumed helmets and ceremonial swords, we are wasting our time.

~

By the way, I also hate these white plastic bracelets people are wearing – "Make Poverty History" or the breast cancer ribbons and prostate brooches, etc. Little signs of solidarity meaning, "I *care*." If you could get a badge saying "Make Poverty Quieter," I might be tempted.

~

Anna and Tristan back after three weeks – just as well as I was getting so plastered and lonely I accessed Friends Reunited. Nobody responded, possibly because in the section where you had to write about yourself I typed, "Look me up in *Who's Who*, sad loser bastards." The children I grew up with are now variously van drivers and supermarket checkout supervisors. A pair of high-fliers became a dentist in Caerphilly and a police superintendent in Swansea.

~

Talking of *Who's Who*, they have an impressive satire or bullshit monitor on the team, as my attempt to add my appearance on *The Bernie Clifton Show* to my list of achievements was disallowed.

~

Off we went to Bigbury to join my in-laws the Dickens clan at their bungalow. The neighbour complained that the children were still playing cricket in the garden at quarter to nine at night. As Nanoo said, "When Mrs Bill lived there she'd invite the children in to watch television and she had cream carpets."

~

It was impossible to find a decent restaurant in Devon. Nobody has had the wit to follow Rick Stein's example and cook fresh local fish, or indeed cook anything. The main eatery in Kingsbridge is called Balti Towers. So we flew to Salzburg again. I'm so obese I couldn't get the tray table down in Economy.

~

Sitting in Café Sissy, Bad Ischl, I forgot that I should have been sitting in seat H39 in the stalls at the National Theatre watching Michael Gambon remember his lines in *Henry IV Parts I and 2*. I didn't feel a single pang of regret. I'm happy to be here. You'd all love the Café Sissy, named not as you might fear for chaps with a marcelled wave in their silver hair, but after Franz-Josef's bride, the Kaiserin Elisabeth, who was stabbed in the heart by an Italian anarchist on Lake Geneva in 1898. Her bloodstained punctured corset is on view in a glass case in the Kaiservilla. It had been a baneful life – Sissy was the mother of Crown Prince Rudolf, who notoriously committed suicide at Mayerling. Ava Gardner plays her in the film. The Café Sissy, with its butterscotch-coloured marble staircase and mosaic floors, the dustclouds drifting from the pale green damask curtains, and with the Ischlers silently munching chocolate pastry in the gloom, is an elegy for Lost Europe – a place of ravaged, desperate nobility. Try keeping me out.

～

The actors I want to see playing Falstaff are Timothy Spall and Ricky Tomlinson, in that order.

～

Didn't attend Penguin's Seventieth Party, as I had to watch *Coronation Street* – Sunita loses her patience with Dev and Bev and Liz go for a drink in the Rovers.

～

First Christmas catalogue received, August 24th.

September
Delivered a talk to the English-Speaking Union in a church hall in Ledbury. A spectacular and brilliant success thoroughly enjoyed by the nine people present. As a result

attempts were made to rope me into addressing the Malvern Rotarians and the English-Speaking Union, Worcester branch. Turned them down. It's the thin edge of the wedge. You'd end up as Ned Sherrin.

~

The Life and Death of Peter Sellers is nominated for a bumper 16 Emmys. The ghastly people at the production company, who didn't even invite me to the premiere of my own film, didn't invite me to any of the awards ceremonies or events, either. "Hopefully Roger will be cheering us on from his living room and we'll all have something to celebrate come Monday," the head of publicity, Fishface Wetwipe*, e-mailed my agent. I had to sit with Fishface in a car to Shepperton once and all she could talk about was getting her hair done.

~

In point of actual fact, Roger was busy laying a curse on all concerned and I'm delighted at the disaster one of the studios involved are having with *Rome*. "Eat these goat testicles. It'll put oak in your penis." The ghost of Anthony Burgess could have provided the dialogue, it's so bad.

~

Offered the honour of a Visiting Professorship at the University of Central England — though how often will I have to visit? — and also offered a free doctorate from the University of Hertfordshire for my "Published Works" —

---

* Still not her real name.

though if you see what some of the reviewers keep saying about my "Published Works" it's not a doctorate I need but an exorcist. The University of Hertfordshire is an institution of learning hitherto unknown to me.

October

Tristan's girlfriend's eighteenth. A black-tie do, to replicate his grand ball. I nearly had a heart attack-cum-stroke when, upon going up to the bar and asking for a very large red wine indeed, the barman said, "That'll be £4.95." This was a new experience for me, paying for drinks at a private party. We later received a bill for £18 from Hannah-Susannah's mother on behalf of the photographer who waylaid and papped us on the way in. The gall of some people. Tristan's girlfriend is now his ex-girlfriend.

~

Back to Bad Ischl for half-term. Austria gorgeous in its autumn colours – deep golds and fiery orange. Our tiny flatlet above a dirndl shop was advertised as *Ideal als Ferienwohnung oder als Alterwohnsitz*, which I think translates as apartment suitable for holidaying widow of an SS officer who has a cat. Luckily the swastika-shaped rotating ceiling fan was gone and the swastika-shaped sunken bath had been filled in by the time we took possession.

~

Alarmed to catch sight of myself in the full-length mirror in the bathroom. It was as if I was in *A Christmas Carol* and Andrea Dworkin was appearing to me out of the mist as one of the ghosts. Physically I resemble a fat lesbian and I could go on a *Newsnight Review Special* on lesbian art and the producers and Mark Lawson wouldn't bat an eyelid.

~

Coming back through Stansted I overheard a woman say, "Ray is very big in the International Caravanning Club" – and the thought of what that might mean made me want to kill myself laughing. Which reminds me – Sue Jones at Food for All, the Christian bookshop here in Bromyard, told me she'd been to a caravan exhibition. I asked "Was it at Earl's Court or the NEC?" She said, "No, the Royal Academy." She meant Caravaggio. Serves me right.

~

Cooked eighty chicken drumsticks for the "Tanzanight," advertised as being "an authentic Tanzanian experience". There was indeed almost an authentic famine, as I underestimated how long it would all take and the food wasn't delivered to Bromyard's Public Hall (known as The Pubic because somebody stole the letter L) in nearly enough time. As the soon-past-its-sell-by-date chicken wasn't thoroughly grilled, I was in danger of poisoning dozens of old ladies, of whom several of the luckier ones would still be clinging to life weeks later. As I said to Anna, all we needed was to let loose a cloud of tsetse flies and get Richard Curtis to come in looking concerned and the authentic African experience would be complete.

November

Our furniture arrived from Canada, where it has been in storage for two years, and was put in storage again, in Ledbury. It has cost vastly more to transport this damn gear around the world than it cost to buy in the first place. I prayed for the container ship to sink – instead there was a cyclone in Birmingham. I am now hoping the warehouse will burn down. My Inverness cape and fifty-seven boxes of books have been dispatched to Austria, again at hilarious expense.

~

A rare trip to London, for a lock-in at the Garrick with Tarquin Olivier and a bunch of old hack chums. Oysters and champagne, lamb cutlets and gallons of claret, and then brandy. Why don't I go the whole hog and wear a curly eighteenth-century wig and get carried about in a sedan chair?

~

A woman in Looby's office is planning on leaving her husband because "his penis is too big." It takes a woman to find such a thing a *burden* and not an *asset*. I said to Anna, "Tell her to try it sunny-side up. Whilst you're about it, get his phone number for Duncan Fallowell."*

~

Oscar is grounded again, until February 2006. He said that "a man" had bought him and his friends a bottle of vodka in

* Divorce ensued. (2009)

Tenbury Wells. But it turned out that Oscar himself was that "man".

~

I receive a letter from a reader about the Queen Mother. Apparently she was not the daughter of Lord Glamis but the daughter of "an unknown Irish labourer." This seems eccentric information, even by the standards of *Daily Express* readers. I must ask Hugo Vickers what he makes of it.

~

A poster in Hereford, "Do Hugs Not Drugs", made me want to take up the crackpipe as soon as I got home.

December

To Austria for the *Adventmarkt* and the *Chriskindlmarkt* and all the other things they do for the holiday season, such as playing Beethoven's "Ode to Joy" on a milking machine (by blowing into it). Being Welsh I consider this a sophisticated accomplishment. Bad Ischl under snow. The streets lined with decorated Christmas trees and lanterns – all of which would be merrily vandalized in two minutes in Britain. Tristan had an afternoon of snowboarding in the Dachstein Mountains. Drinking mulled wine next to the log fires in the town square, wearing my father's old coat, I was almost happy. Then the snow turned to rain.

2006

January

ANGUISH AGAIN! Back from Austria Anna discovered two
points on her licence and a cyst on her ovary. Sexual intercourse has thus had to take a bit of a back seat this year.
She's also had so many speeding fines that this time she was
up before the beak and faced with disqualification. Though
the camera had caught her doing but 34 mph in a 30-mph
zone, the latest offence did take place in fairness outside
The Royal National College For The Blind, hence not considered a laughing matter except by me. I didn't attend the
court as any Ironside intervention would have meant
several years in the poky, and anyway Anna got herself off.
She really should have been a lawyer. She'd have got Hitler
off. Instead of which she does whatever she does for the
abused and troubled children of Worcestershire for hardly
any money, and the educational psychology department of
Worcestershire County Council is so highly regarded its
people have to share desks with colleagues from as it might
be the Environmental Health Helpline (pest control/lost
and stray dogs). And don't get me on to the subject of my

own *mortifyingly bad pay*. I published over eighty articles this year in the national press and would have been better rewarded washing the tables down in Mrs Muffin's Tea Shoppe, Ledbury. Whenever I ask a posturing turd at a newspaper for an adjustment in my fee I'm told (always over an expensive lunch) that they wish they could help, but these are difficult times and their hands are tied, advertising revenue is down, etc. I've been getting the same speech since going up to Magdalen in 1982. Why I'm not as famous as Sandi Toksvig I'll never know.

February

A few years ago the Hobbit-featured and scrofulous Humphrey Carpenter nominated me for a Fellowship of the Royal Society of Literature, an august body that holds tea parties in the Strand to discuss Robert Browning. A letter arrived from the secretary saying that as I'd been resoundingly turned down *four consecutive times* my nomination had now lapsed. Humphrey had threatened to resign from the RSL if I hadn't been elected. Instead he dropped dead. One day I might come to see this as an overreaction. What is it they *want*? What is it I *lack*? It doesn't help that I have at least three sworn enemies on the committee, whose crap books I have publicly vilified. But a bottomless humiliation – and frankly is it any blessed wonder that Lucy Ellmann has put me in one of her novels (cleverly disguised as a character called Roger Lewis) with sinister veracity as a person who is driven to mass murder out of sheer frustration and lack of recognition? Inside my head Bernard Herrmann's stabbing music from *Psycho* is pulsating non-freaking-stop. My much-loved pen-pal Paul Bailey (a spry Hart-Davis to my bilious George Lyttelton) says he'll re-nominate me. We'll see.*

I was, however, elected to the Garrick, so resigned the same day. This was because they refused to allow me Country Membership, stipulating that one has to live 150 miles from the club to qualify for the cheaper subscription. Bromyard is 148 miles from the club. I said what about if I stand at the end of the garden or on the roof? Letters were also addressed to me in Hertfordshire instead of Herefordshire, which implied they were a bit confused. A few chaps I know are Country Members and they don't live 150 miles from the club, unless Sussex and Hampshire have floated off to sea, like the bandstand in the Marx Brothers' *At the Circus*.

March

Anna to the county hospital, sensibly leaving nothing to chance and going by bus. To put it succinctly, she underwent a bilateral oophorectomy or in veterinary parlance the old girl had to be spayed. Which parenthetically rather begs the question how can one tell if an Airedale is having a hot flush? We spent an anxious week waiting for the biopsy reports and I kept myself amused by mugging up on how to

*He never did. Lynne Truss and Kathryn Hughes did fill in the forms but haven't got anywhere either. (2009)

apply for my Disability Attendance Carer's Allowance. Basically I'll be paid more for Anna's ovaries than I get from reviewing books for the *Daily Telegraph*. The leaflets one finds on display in the women's health ward incidentally show what's on the horizon – Help the Aged publications on *Bladder and Bowel Weakness*, *Fitter Feet* and (my favourite) *Staying Steady*.

April

I see in the riveting Court Circular that The Princess Royal, President of the Patrons, Crime Concern, made a visit to Merthyr Tydfil Youth Inclusion Project at Cyfarthfa Castle Museum and Art Gallery, Brecon Road, Merthyr Tydfil, and was received by Her Majesty's Lord-Lieutenant of Mid Glamorgan (a Mrs Kathrin [sic] Thomas). Her Royal Highness later visited the Multi-Discipline Intervention Service, Torfaen, Woodlands, Mamhilad Business Park, Pontypool, and was received by Her Majesty's Lord-Lieutenant of Gwent (a Mr Simon Boyle). The Princess Royal later visited Dragon Bands, Pontypool Industrial Estate, Pontnewynydd, Pontypool. Her Royal Highness afterwards visited the Clarence Regeneration Project at the Clarence Hotel, Clarence Corner, Pontypool. The Princess Royal later attended a Foster Carers' Celebration at Caerphilly Castle.

Nothing much happened to me, but it was certainly all go for Princess Anne.

SEASONAL SUICIDE NOTES

May

As I am now a visiting professor at the (don't you *dare* fucking laugh) University of Central England in Birmingham*, I get asked to address various well-meaning groups. So to Ledbury to open the Ledbury Poetry Festival with a lecture appropriately enough entitled "What is poetry?" My audience consisted of Private Godfrey's sister Dolly and her two dozen identical chums, i.e. lots of smiling old ladies in brown lace who used to know John Masefield personally. Afterwards I was asked to sign as many as three copies of my books. When *Mister Jesus* comes out these are the very ladies who'll smother me to death in a dark lane with a sponge cake.

~

The first Christmas catalogue arrived on May 30th – *Viva: New Ideas for Health and Well-Being*. But why are the models who model the bunion correction pads, knee braces, posture support devices and down-filled booties so young, happy and smiling with such bright white teeth? By rights these products should be advertised by the coffin-dodging folk they are intended for – demented bearded ladies, sour pensioners with haemorrhoids and tartan shopping bags, the arthritic and the morbidly obese. Gainful employment for our beloved housekeeper! Nevertheless, except for Sandi

---

*Previously the City of Birmingham College of Commerce, then the North Birmingham Technical College, after that a poly of some description and currently or anyway momentarily, Birmingham City University.

Toksvig who'll get a pogo stick in her stocking as usual, all my future present-giving problems are solved by *The Whiz*.

A breakthrough in comfort & convenience for women

Now there's no way to describe this revolutionary idea without discussing natural bodily functions, so please bear with us. When you don't want to sit on an unsanitary public toilet or when you have to go outdoors – or if you find it hard to squat down or hover – use the Whiz ®. This ingenious British invention enables women to urinate in a standing position. Called a 'urine director', it has a cleverly-designed 'lily shield' shape that fits snugly against the groin. Once you start nature and gravity do the rest; urine is directed away from the body so there ar no splashes or accidents. You don't even have to remove outer or underclothing. The Whiz® is made from a high-grade thermoplastic elastomer, impregnated with anti-bacterial and anti-fungal agents for hygiene. Folds to carry in pocket or bag. Rinses clean in seconds. 6" (15cm) long.

48313 The Whiz® £7.95

June – The big time. I talked to the Malvern Rotary Club about Laurence Olivier. Hugely magnanimous, I eschewed any fee and requested that instead the Malvern Rotarians made a donation to Tarquin Olivier's Laurence Olivier Statue Fund. A big bronze Larry is to be unveiled next year by Richard Attenborough outside the National, at a cost of £10,000 or £100,000, anyway a lot. Well a few weeks later Tarquin wrote to me saying he'd mysteriously received a cheque from the Malvern Rotarians for £25. So that's what I'm worth on the after-dinner speaking circuit is it? What another crying humiliation. Even Sandi Toksvig will command more than that. As for the Laurence Olivier statue, the Malvern Rotarians will be lucky to have just about paid for one of the bolts that will hold the thing down.

July

Yet again Faber do not invite me to their Summer Party, even though I review dozens of their pretentious books and they hold the rights to several of my own celebrated ravings. I wouldn't go of course, but that's not the point. So imagine how happy it made me to learn that because so many of my former editors are in and out of The Priory, screaming and tearing off their clothes and walking into walls with a saucepan on their head, The Roger Lewis Mentally Handicapped Publishers' Wing is already at the advanced planning stage. In any case publishers don't want literature any longer. All they want to do is sell Jordan's tits in Tesco, I kid you not.

August – Several weddings, which I never enjoy. I wondered why this was. The fat bridesmaids? The ill-rehearsed theatricality? The forced jollity? The boring speeches? The tedium of the photographers and hanging about for the drinks? None of these. I hate weddings because I'm not the centre of attention.

~

The children get their results. Oh Christ. Oscar got a handful of C-grades and revealed that he's had a tattoo done. Tattoos are all right for sailors, gypsies and the strongman at the circus, but not for the nice middle-class sons of a Professor from the University of Central England and a Faber author so distinguished Faber dare not invite him to their summer parties for fear he'll eclipse DBC Pierre. As for Tristan – this is truly hard to believe. After three terms at Hereford Sixth Form College went down the toilet and two further easy-going years doodling at Herefordshire College of Art and Design (known by me contemptuously as The Colouring-In College) he still managed to fail his diploma. How in the name of Satan's Portion can one fail *art* in *Hereford*? This is a unique and virtually Dada-ist achievement worthy of an A-star-grade and a round of applause from the shades of Marcel Duchamp and André Breton. He also failed Film Studies by sleeping through the exam. So he approaches his twentieth birthday without real direction, motiveless and still thinking life is free, food and shelter provide by mummy and daddy. Well why not.

~

To Austria to run up my cake slate at Zauner's. Anna and I are now so fat our 1982 wedding photo fell off the wall. Much boredom and inconvenience at Stansted, where owing to high security alerts sweet Home Counties grandmas and babies in pushchairs are flung against the breezeblocks and strip-searched by armed guards. One wants to scream out that I'm not the Taliban! *I'm not a hook-nosed sodomitical camel-fucker from Al-Queda!* But instead we meekly put up with it and terrorists continue to get away with it. True to form Anna got a speeding ticket from the Salzburg police. The frightening-looking Germanic bluster on the charge sheet resembled an edict from the Nazi high command. All they actually wanted was a 70 euro fine.

~

Time for a joke, courtesy of Paul Bailey's personal fish-monger, Phil the Fish, of Turnham Green. A class of schoolchildren is talking about morals – discussing the meaning of "Don't put all your eggs in one basket," "Don't count your chickens before they are hatched," and so forth. One pupil then says about his Auntie Sharon, who is a fighter pilot in Helmand Province. She crash lands. She walks away from the plane, a bottle of Scotch in one hand, a machine gun in the other, a machete between her teeth. A hundred Taleban warriors are watching. She necks the Scotch in its entirety. Shoots eighty Taleban. Chops up the other twenty. "But what's the moral ?" bleats the teacher. *"Don't fuck with my Auntie Sharon when she's been drinking,"* comes the reply. Obvious when you think of it.

September – A big box arrived from California containing a framed and glazed Certificate from the Academy of Television Arts and Sciences "honoring" me for my contribution to the Primetime Emmy in the Best Adapted Screenplay category. I thought this a hoax perpetrated by John Betjeman's definitive if testy biographer Bevis Hillier, on a roll after sabotaging his ebullient if slapdash rival A.N. Wilson's John Betjeman biography. I wrote to the president of the Academy of Television Arts and Sciences, informing them that somebody had stolen their stationery and was running amok with a word-processor and a photocopier, distributing fake Emmys to the gullible and susceptible. But no – a polite letter came back from the senior vice president (awards) insisting that I "enjoy the well-deserved recognition." Now the thing is this refers to the 2004-2005 ceremonies. You'd have thought somebody from the vast contingent of executive producers might have mentioned it to me before now. But then look at the way Hollywood treated Maria Von Trapp, cutting her dead and deliberately forgetting to ask her to the premiere of *The Sound of Music*, and so forth. Who'd ever have thought I'd have anything in common with Maria Von Trapp?

October
To Paris, where Tristan is living in Montmartre with a tap

dancer called Amy Tortue, an existence that should be depicted by Lautrec. Anna's parents came with us. I asked Anna's mother, "How's Aunty Pawsey? I heard she was going senile." "She's had new carpets throughout," was the bewildering reply. Anna and I stayed at the five-star Hotel Astor and we put the in-laws and Oscar and Sébastien up round the corner in what was probably once a cheap brothel known to Mata Hari.

~

Jack Straw is in hot water for saying Muslim women shouldn't go around dressed in parachutes, trussed up like chickens and concealed from view. I personally think the veil should be made compulsory in Wales, for if there is such a thing as an attractive Welshwoman I'm a Dutchman. Squat midgets – most of them my relatives, so I speak with authority. I'm writing a definitive book on this subject called *Ratbags and Sleazeballs*, part of *The Kill Fees Trilogy*.

November

Friends from the Players Club, New York, are handing in their dinner pails. Patrick Tull's gruff sarcastic exterior never successfully concealed his gruff sarcastic interior. He was once a Welsh chef on *Crossroads* and had appeared in *Peter Pan* when Alastair Sim was Captain Hook. "What was Alastair Sim like?" I asked eagerly. "As you'd expect," said Patrick – which must rank as the world's least revealing theatrical anecdote ever. The Players is full of old darlings who haven't worked for decades. When one of them got a job recently as a corpse in *The Sopranos* he disconcerted James Gandolfini by asking, "What is my motivation in this scene?"

~

The best things about The Players for me were always the wraiths and old crocks with their stories. I'd be in seventh heaven listening to the chap who'd been Rex Harrison's understudy in *My Fair Lady* tell me how he "went through eleven Eliza Doolittles." I met the woman who voiced Betty Boop and the ancient party who'd been attacked by W.C.

**Typical South Welsh beauty:
Nurse Margaret Thomas of Machen**

Fields with an ice-pick, when he was Babe LeRoy. Years ago with George Nestor I encountered a wizened fellow who said he'd been John Barrymore's stage manager during the Broadway run of *Hamlet*. Apparently the curtain went up to reveal everyone in Claudius's court rolling around in their velvet codpieces, drunk on goblets of Rhenish and Mosel wines. As they groped each other under their fur-lined gowns, the tense and peculiar Prince sat off to one side in profile, gazing into the flickering fireplace as if posing for a portrait by John Singer Sargent.

As it was always generally believed that Shakespeare wrote the play with Barrymore expressly in mind, I wondered what Barrymore used to say his motivation was, regarding Hamlet's attitude towards Claudius and Gertrude? What were the deep psychological undercurrents? The long-retired stage manager said Barrymore was always asked this. "That red-bearded prick is putting his cock up my mother's cunt every night!" was the actor's stock response. I said that doesn't sound like something they'd teach you at the RADA. "No, but there was always a green light on the ghost – and, when Hamlet interrogates Gertrude later in the play, Barrymore made the bit with his mother into a passionate love scene. The same green light shone on him, as if he was being impelled by his father's spirit."

Not one critic noticed this – it was before everyone else's Freudian interpretations. Barrymore said that the ghost was "the sort of stupid bastard whose wife was bound to cheat on him out of sheer ennui." John Barrymore used to love coming to London for the fogs. He died in 1942.

December

My first trip to London since the Gladstone administration and I set up operational HQ in that epicentre of modern world culture, the Groucho (Country Member @ £300 a year), where it was suddenly quarter-past-five in the morning and I was drinking brandy with Irish film directors and the actor Cillian Murphy. The veteran character actor Jonathan Cecil and myself were complaining about the disappointing uselessness of Series 2 of *Extras* – where the characters and story were no longer credible; where there was too much reliance on the gimmick of a big star; where lovely Ashley Jensen was given nothing to do – when naturally who should get up from behind us but Ricky Gervais. He went to order something at the bar and the barman (who knows who I am) didn't know who he was. "It's Gervais – G,E,R,V,A,I,S," he said whilst blinking a lot and believing himself to be the victim of a confidence trick. A splendid end to my year.

2007

January

AS COLERIDGE USED TO SAY – "So completely has a whole year passed, with scarcely the fruits of a *month* – Oh! Sorrow & Shame! I have done nothing." Except nearly one hundred articles, for which I continue to be humiliatingly badly paid and that get to be cut to accommodate advertisements for Allied Carpets – as if there is a conspiracy to make me look clumsy and illiterate. On the home front and to my mingled shame/horror/amusement I discover that the children have been telling their friends that the fat complaining character shuffling about the place when they call is a Lithuanian asylum seeker working half-heartedly as the maid – and their friends have been believing this without demur. "Oh don't bother about *her*." Indeed – I'd believe it myself, should I be in their position. There was an alarming photo in the *Hereford Times*, which I thought was illustrating a feature about the disappearing barn owl. It turned out on investigation to be a picture of me – plucked and stuffed and with the expression of a man with a spear in his back.

~

A New Year's Day Party at Anna's brother's mansion, about which I was correct to have misgivings. Three boring hours there and three boring hours back. "If anybody asks me when we arrive if I'd like tea or coffee I'll be as mad as a meat-axe," I said – not my exact words. "Would you like tea or coffee?" I was asked when we arrived. The children looked at me expectantly – and I stood there with a silly grin all over my silly face. Other grown up members of the family take boiled rice or melon balls to these parties. I contribute a *forced gaiety*.

~

The big news in Bromyard is that Age Concern "suffered a cruel setback" when somebody stole their kettle.

February
The editor of a local newspaper came to see me and got every fact it is possible to get wrong wrong. Martin Sheen is the actor who played Blair and Kenneth Williams. Pinter's famous play was *The Carpenter*. I said that Albert Camus was a comical French detective and he agreed with me.

~

My financial services advisor's nephew Perci-Preece who some time ago dyed his hair pink has announced that he drops anchor in Poo Bay. Mrs Troll reflected, having given this some serious thought, "But one thing you can say for them, they are always *very kind*, aren't they?"

~

The good news is that a woman in Hereford has been able to

smell and taste a banana for the first time in thirty years. "Smoker Alison Smith decided to give up with unexpected results. She can now smell and taste bananas and her life has taken on a whole new meaning."

~

My birthday and Sébastien was home with the earache and I had to sit with him in the doctors with all the spluttering old folk. The bank phoned at 9.31 precisely to say I was overdrawn and so or hence they wouldn't be paying my annual Legal and General life insurance premium. So I'm not even allowed to *die*. Then one of my teeth fell out and I had to go to the fang bandit and spit blood into a bowl. It was my birthday and I was visibly – indeed cartoonishly – disintegrating before my loved ones. The only thing to keep me going was reading in the *Hereford Times* that eighty-one-year-old pensioner Joan Wheeler of Flax Place, off the Pershore Road in Upton Snodsbury, died after she "tripped over her cat, an inquest heard. A verdict of accidental death was recorded." But what happened to the cat? I do worry about such loose ends. It can keep me wide awake at night.

March

If you are meant to suffer for your art then after me David Howard is the next Orson Welles. Seven years ago he sent me the first of many drafts for a poetic zombie film he'd written called *Flick*. In my capacity as acting unpaid self-appointed literary advisor, I'd send back pages of comments and generally helped keep up morale, my vested interest being the hope that one day Howard will make a biopic of my Charles Hawtrey book, bringing to the topic a visual style that might best be described as Old Mother Riley on acid. I want Hawtrey to be played by Mackenzie Crook.

Howard goes in for wonky camera angles, deep focus long shadows, and vivid neon lights. (It could be the inside of my head.) The screen constantly dissolves and shifts, leaves fall in slow motion, birds flap in gilded cages – and that's when he's making a promo for Welsh rugby. *Flick* was to be a homage to Fifties B-movies, saturated with comic book greens and yellows, as if the celluloid had been left in the Technicolor bath too long. Set against the backdrop of a seedy dance hall and the rock'n'roll music scene, the plot alluded to the song-of-love-and-death revenge formula – as when disfigured Vincent Price's Dr Phibes rises again or Vincent Price as Edward Lionheart kills off the critics in *Theatre of Blood*, young Johnny Flick comes back from the dead to slice up the school bullies and reclaim the girl of his dreams, jive queen Sally Andrews, who by this time has metamorphosed from Hayley Angel Wardle into Sixties babe Julia Foster.

Though the total budget was to be less than a third of what Tom Cruise's trailer-caravan costs, it took David and his scrummy business partner Rik Hall an age to organise the finances, utilising what Sellers used to call brown paper and string. But today cameras are finally rolling and so I'm visiting the location in Newbridge, in the coalmining valleys near Pontypool. A shuttered and crumbling Art

Deco working men's institute has been dressed as a night-club for the opening scene, with a rotating giant glitter ball, torn velvet seats and broken stained glass windows.

The local comprehensive school has been taken over for the dancers and extras to get into their costumes – selections are made from racks of swirling skirts and Teddy Boy gear, gleaned from charity shops. Queues of youngsters wait patiently for a hairdresser to spray them with lacquer to create beehives and quiffs. Oscar is amongst the throng. He's been on set for two days and in the finished print he's a silhouette in the far distance, glimpsed for a microsecond.

As I'd said to David, "get plenty of dwarves. Fill the screen with dwarves. You can't go wrong with dwarves," a mother and daughter midget duo were to be seen perfecting their attire in the make-up area, trying on high-heels. Oscar got chatting to Hob and Knob as we affectionately called them, and apparently they've already been in many of the Harry Potter movies, and they once played the dinosaurs in *Barney*. "She was the blue one and I was the yellow one. But the phone don't go often for extra work because we do stand out," they said sadly. "We have our own agent for people under five-foot." I enquired if they'd ever worked with Martin Amis. "Who's he?" they asked.

The trick with extra work is to try and loom into shot, elbow your way to the front line. A girl (David's sister) blatantly sat on Oscar's lap, obscuring him from view, and after a dozen or so takes, bugger me if the dwarves weren't hogging the lens, as if the scene where Johnny Flick runs amok with his knife was actually meant to be about them. I heard later that there were creative differences over this or other matters – and Hob and Knob threatened the director with a summons for their unpaid taxi fare of £12.50. "They'll take you to the Small Claims Court," I said, the only wisecrack I have ever knowingly made.

Central to the film was the role of Memphis cop Lieutenant Annie McKenzie, to be played by Faye Dunaway. It seemed such a surreal image – Academy Award-winning Hollywood icon Faye Dunaway in Pontypool. But it had happened here or hereabouts before. Sophia Loren and Gregory Peck once clambered across the Crumlin viaduct in *Arabesque*, Ingrid Bergman walked the Black Mountains with Burt Kwouk, pretending to be a missionary escaping from China in *The Inn of the Sixth Happiness*, and the sainted Charles Hawtrey's Private Widdle guarded the Khyber Pass at Llanberis. Local pubs and cafes still have wrinkled signed souvenir snaps to prove this.

But Faye's involvement had more parallels with my auntie Bette Davis coming to Britain in camp old age to make horror pics such as *The Nanny*, Joan Crawford appearing in *Trog* and Joan Fontaine as Alec McCowen's devil-worshipping sister in *The Witches*. Despite such Grand Guignol precedents, one of Howard's main achievements nevertheless is that he was to get Faye to give one of her few non-mental performances. Her American policewoman is unusually warm-hearted, sassy and tolerant. Perhaps her co-star helped out here. During her majestic career Faye has worked with Steve McQueen, Paul Newman, Marlon Brando, Robert Redford, Jack Nicholson, Johnny Depp – and now, er, Mark Benton, who plays McKenzie's sidekick, burly and jovial Sergeant Miller (see p82). "Faye learned a lot from me," he confessed – and maybe he wasn't joking.

With Mrs Troll and her many in-need-of-the-burqua stunt doubles at large, we are used to feisty dames in the Principality (Dorothy Squires, Jean Rhys, Rachel Roberts, Elizabeth Taylor on her visits to Pontrydyfen), but old Faye took the biscuit. People found her fragile and frantic, hard-edged, and licked by Hellfire, with her arched eyebrows and shining lips. There's a scene in the film with a little old lady propped up in bed – she's overheard one of the murders and McKenzie comes to have a word. The little old lady in the script was an old bloke. Windsor Davies and Victor Spinetti being unaccountably unavailable, Howard cast Margaret John*, who only the previous day had come out of the Heath Hospital. She fell fast asleep in bed on the set, "and when I came to, there's Faye Dunaway staring at me." Margaret thought she'd genuinely died and expected to be prodded by a pitchfork.

Perfectionist Faye's first tantrum had to do with finding a cable for her computer. Eventually she was able to laugh it off a little, exclaiming, "If anybody *dared* behave like this to *me*!" It helped (or hindered) that nobody in PC World in

---

*Margaret has since found greater fame as the sex-mad geriatric and Barry Island neighbour in *Gavin and Stacey*.

Cardiff knew who the golly heck she was. In Pontypool she had to change into her costume in the Public Toilets, and when she emerged in black glasses and with a towel wrapped around her head, again no passerby gave her a second glance. *Bonnie and Clyde* was evidently a long while ago.

Bearing the brunt of her ire was her assistant, Angharad. "Ang-*har-ad*!" became a familiar yell, reminiscent of "*Christina*! Fetch me an *axe*!" It was one of Angharad's jobs to write out Faye's dialogue on huge sheets of paper and sellotape these around the set, taking care not to disturb the other actors' eye-lines. I asked Liz Smith, my favourite actress in the world, how it went.

Liz plays Johnny's mother, who lives in a time-warp flat decorated with mildewy wallpaper, behind which we can imagine bodies are hidden, as in Reginald Christie's abode at Rillington Place. For the role of Ma, Liz had further perfected her trademark look of distant eccentricity, singing to herself as she launders blood-stained shirts and watches a kettle bubble and screech on the filthy stove. She is also nagging and shrill, with a clinging protectiveness towards her Johnny.

"I did enjoy the madness of it, blended with the music," she told me. "My character loves her son totally, but she has no concept of the passage of time – she doesn't realise he's dead. Timeless she is, and will wait for him forever. He's risen from the dead and all she's worried about is whether he'll catch cold or wants a cup of tea. She's in her own world altogether. A mad dream." Yes – but Faye Dunaway?

"Total hell. Dreadful. Played up every single moment. She wrote her lines on these great pieces of paper! She was snotty, she was. The big star! Very nice to me, though."

Honorary Welshwoman Faye would be used to such comments. She's been through it before a hundred times, most notably with my auntie Bette Davis no less in a NBC-TV movie called *The Disappearance of Aimee*. One of Bette's more inventive complaints was that Faye spent her evenings riding around Denver in a limo drinking champagne. There have also been well-documented battles with Roman Polanski – Faye allegedly got so cross with him during *Chinatown*, she peed in a glass and tipped it over his head. (If she didn't – she should've!) She herself explains

Mark Benton, Margaret John and Faye Dunaway in *Flick*

away such rage by saying that, in the acting profession, fighting is a required skill. "If you fold, if you let yourself bend, you will not make it, truly make it. You have to defend yourself from the assaults of others."

With Liz Smith, in a small way, there was a battle for power. When Mark Benton made Liz laugh during a take, Faye was furious. "Don't do that to a Dame of England for Chrissakes!" During the effing and blinding we seriously started to wonder if Faye had been assuming Liz Smith was actually Dame Maggie Smith? Yet for all the diva antics — juggling three mobile phones, fussing all day with her curling tongs and causing delays — it wasn't Faye who wanted to change hotels or who the day before the shoot started threatened to back out. It was Liz. "I don't like working on location," she said. David had to explain that her scenes would be in a nice warm studio.

Also, where were Lynda Baron and Shirley Ann Field? Despite the tight budget, Lynda wanted more money and a better expenses deal, which was not feasible without re-negotiating everyone's contracts. So she was replaced by Anna Karen, the immortal Olive from *On the Buses* — which was infuriating for the producers, as in the flashback scenes a young Lynda Baron lookalike (Katherine Judkins) had been found. Shirley Ann Field wanted equal billing with Faye Dunaway. So she was replaced by Julia Foster. "I had the script at twelve, accepted the role at two, had the wig fitted and at three started shooting. I hadn't acted for nine years."

～

Sheridan Morley has died. What a ghastly old hack he was, who always went out of his way to give me nasty reviews. The Brian Blessed of theatre reviewing, bellowing and snorting and cultivating a serious beard. He once greeted Paul Bailey by breezily inquiring, "Hello Paul. Anything in the typewriter?" However, what a good title for a collection of journalism, *Anything in the Typewriter*? Then I was invited to his memorial service, so I felt (momentarily) guilty about thinking he was a fat talentless idiot and a waste of the planet's oxygen.

~

Ian Richardson also drops dead. The mainspring of his performances was suppressed, vinegary camp. When Ian Bannen's understudy had to take over as Hamlet, Ian Richardson who was playing Rosencrantz was most put out – because the understudy whose name was Edgar Longstaff was crap. Edgar Longstaff subsequently had a sex change to become Cynthia Longstaff and lived in Lanzarote as a lesbian.

~

My ex-neighbour Garth is in the thick of Alzheimer's in a home in Oakdale. He gets up and dresses in the middle of the night when the drugs wear off and walks along the ward switching people's notes on the clipboards. He then gets back in the wrong bed and patients end up landing on the floor. "He's been complaining that he lost his stick and the nurses said he never had a stick, but Muriel took a new one in again on Friday, and she's had three types of cancer and is only on £50 a week," said Mrs Troll caringly. NHS hospitals in South Wales are indeed a worry – a rugby player with a neck injury was taken to theatre for a hysterectomy.

April

I saw a lady in a mobile wheelchair in the Co-op examining the detergents, one by one. "I want bleach to smell like bleach when I put it on my dishcloth, not patchouli," she muttered. I said I quite agreed. Do you know you can get Apple and Mango Toilet Duck now – when all you want to do is sluice the bog with it, not make a fucking fruit salad.

~

Anna's Auntie Majolica has died in Suckley. I phoned her son (sixty-seven) a telephone salesman in Wyre Piddle with my condolences. He was so upset he couldn't get any words out. "But she was ninety-two," I said, failing to put on an entirely convincing compassionate voice.

~

Needing as we all do a little light as spilled from heaven, I was tickled when my friend Steve said that Sir Archibald Clerk-Kerr, a former ambassador in Moscow, had a Turkish colleague whose business card said he was called Mustapha Kunt. "We all feel like that now and then, especially when spring is upon us, but few of us would care to put it on our cards. It takes a Turk to do that," said Steve.

~

To France, to see Tristan who is working near Fougères as a group leader at an activity centre place. Zip-wires, archery, quad bikes etc. He tells the children that the frogs which have been used for frogs' legs in the kitchen are fitted with little wheelchairs. Then we went to visit Fatty Prescott*. Fatty and I were Mixed Infants in Mrs Harrington's class many years ago and he has now moved to live in Normandy, where he maintains the gardens of British people's holiday homes. I was taken aback on entering his lounge-room to see many of my heirlooms filling the place – Victorian dressers, mirrors, chairs and pictures. Some of this furniture Anna and I bought in St. Andrews. It turns out that it had been *sold* to him when the various French houses were emptied out after my father's death. I'd have been less outraged if at least it had been freely *given* away – but not to have offered the stuff back to me first... If I was on speaking terms with my mother I'd have asked her to intervene. But, hey, live and let live.

~

Mrs Troll's new friend is her Sat Nav. She shouts back at it and had a huge argument trying to find a wool shop in Llandeilo.

~

* Not *that* Fatty Prescott, i.e. the Right Honourable John ("Peace Be Upon Him") Prescott, the look-you-in-the-eye MP for Hull East and deputy prime minister, but the legendary Nicholas Andrew Prescott, from Upper Machen, South Wales, who when invited to discuss the principles of volcanic activity in his A-level geography paper said in his concluding remarks, "Whoosh, up it goes!" He got a Distinction and a fan letter from the examiners. He proceeded to Swansea University and took a degree in Social Anthropology. He can sink a pint quicker than anyone I've ever seen. The truth of the matter is, these days I'm far fatter than Fatty.

Ex-neighbour Garth has had his stick taken from him because he's been sword fighting with it. He thought he was back doing National Service and the ward was the barracks.

May – I was asked at the last minute to do an *Oldie* lunch at Simpsons. "Who dropped out then?" – "Michael Winner." God knows how many people they'd asked to stand in for Michael Winner before in desperation they got to me – and even I said no. I suggested they call Syd Little, "the clown who made a nation laugh."

~

I have an e-mail stalker, a man with a metal plate in his head in Grimsby. Up to six messages-plus-attachments a day, which I delete unopened. He started as a fan, and then grew familiar, and finally he became aggressive and contemptuous, angrily jealous. He'd send me clippings of my own articles, covered with yellow highlighter pen and teacher-style ticks and crosses. "You only appear in the *Mail on Sunday* so that people on the lavatory in Bedwas will think Lewis the butcher's son has done well." As if thirty years on this is my motivation! Which of course it is. He particularly hates me for knowing famous people – whereas in point of absolute fact my closest proximity to celebrity is that I once had a postcard from Gyles Brandreth, sent with a second class stamp.

~

The first Christmas catalogue arrived on May 15th.

~

At the Bromyard Afternoon Club, the monthly raffle made £18 and the Bring & Buy made £9. At their next meeting Mr Maskell will be talking about his "Memories of Hazardous Chemicals".

June

Worcestershire is full of splendid place-names, many of which inspired P.G.Wodehouse – the parish of Upton Snodsbury with Broughton Hackett and Naunton Beauchamp, for instance, or Grafton Flyford with North Piddle and Flyford Flavell. We went to Upton-on-Severn for a picnic because I'd heard there was a place there called Minge Lane and wanted to be photographed by the sign. There's another beauty spot in Oxford called Crotch Crescent. I saw a strange film later, in which Beryl Reid turned into a frog, the great George Sanders was the butler, Nicky Henson rode a motorbike, and Robert "Tim" Hardy – who though he has often impersonated Winston Churchill would be better still if cast as Edward Heath, a politician who was more Martha than Arthur by the way – as usual stuck out his jaw and pursed his mouth to imply *consternation*. Or did I dream the whole thing up?

~

To *Lord of the Rings* at Drury Lane. It was so bad and portentous I thought Brian Blessed was in it. I couldn't tell if we were meant to be down a mine or up a hill; nor were the characters differentiated – I didn't realise that Aragorn and Legolas, Arwen and Galadriel, and Gandalf and Saruman were not the same person(s). Or whether Lothlorien was a place or a character? I just don't know my Orc from my Ent. Only Asperger's Syndrome sufferers and boys pre-girlfriends like Tolkien – for there's no actual social interaction (it is all battles and set speeches; no eroticism or comedy); everybody exists in stately, rule-bound isolation.

~

In Hereford a woman threw her artificial leg off a bridge into the Wye, "as a desperate plea for help." Vinny Hilton from Hopton Road who lost her real leg to diabetes said she was "totally frustrated" with the way she was being treated – specifically, the Council have yet to fit her stairs with a stair lift, she can only shower "when her husband helps," her wheelchair doesn't fit through the door, and her commode is so "badly designed and unsafe" she has often fallen off, "suffering many bumps and bruises." She also wants somebody to come and do all her housework. What a bone idle miserable, grasping bitch. I hope nobody kindly retrieved her artificial leg and that by now it has floated out to sea. But hats off to her for knowing her way round the benefits system.

July
Our rich friends the Turners have a fancy dress party in Raglan. There were 7 Batman and Robin duos, 5 Jack Sparrows from *Pirates of the Caribbean*, 2 Queen Mothers in plastic tiaras from Suzie's Fancy Dress Shop in Trethomas, 11 Pocohontases, and 268 nuns.

Gyles Brandreth called in for lunch on his way to address the Oswestry branch of Bingo for the Deaf. I asked him if it is true that Sandi Toksvig is an Eskimo? He looked at me askance. I made him a cup of tea. "This is the most wonderful cup of tea I have ever had in my life," he said, so firmly I believed it. I opened the door to the dining room and we proceeded to tuck in. "This is the most wonderful lunch I have ever had in my life," he claimed. Later on, Anna took him to Leominster Railway Station. "This is the most wonderful lift I have ever had in my life," I expected him to say in a heartfelt manner – and when the Arriva Trains Wales train pulled in, "This is the most wonderful train I have ever seen in my life." I suppose up until that very precise moment, such sentiments may well be true – and if from minute to minute and day to day you manage to exist positively and continuously in the present tense, they'll always be true. For myself, I can never stop being overwhelmed by the past and see only fiasco and anticlimax in prospect.

Nevertheless, being as Gyles is keen for the next experience and pouncing as Gyles does upon the instant must allow for an extraordinary freedom: "The life where hope and memory are as one," as Wordsworth or Coleridge or Byron or one of those skylark-loving-daffodil-waving characters in a flouncy blouse put it. I'm dead envious.*

The last time a celebrity visited Bromyard was in 1964 when Princess Margaret attended a church service, so this was a red letter day indeed. We nearly had game-for-a-laugh Lynn Barber here once. There was to be a family wedding in the vicinity and she'd hoped to witness her brother-in-law (was it?) in his speech consistently and faultlessly confuse the names of his own wife Angela with her prettier younger sister Pamela (was it?), easy enough to do when you're tongue-tied and a bag of nerves, but don't expect ever to be completely forgiven. But Lynn chucked.

~

I must be Gyles's idea of a total nightmare – an Oxford-educated prize-winning man-of-letters living in seclusion and obscurity and in such penury I don't have a pot to piss in nor an unmortgaged window to throw it out of. Gyles by contrast owns a castle in SW13 with turrets and battlements – indeed, I think he *owns* SW13. What a versatile and ubiquitous character Gyles is – I'm lost in admiration: the television presenting and speeches; the radio quiz shows and panel games; his books and diary collections; he's been an MP and playwright, has appeared in West End musicals and is an expert on the royal family, where he is the official gazetted Fool to Prince Philip's Lear; his exceptional novels about Oscar Wilde-as-Sherlock Holmes might well be filmed with Stephen Fry or

---

* Julian Fellowes, the Heinrich Himmler of Social Etiquette, has said that "being a Good Guest is a performing art." If this is then the case, Gyles is surely in the Sarah Bernhardt class. When you have his attention – to quote from his very own novel, *Oscar Wilde and the Dead Man's Smile*, "He charmed me in the way that all charmers do: he made me feel that I was the only person that mattered to him." I'm always too psychically or temperamentally cluttered to pull this off myself; too contrary and ironic and brooding; too blinking *Welsh*. (2009)

possibly Gerard Depardieu... What does this all suggest to you – many-sidedness and a quicksilver brain, or restlessness and blind panic? I have never met Mrs Gyles, but I envisage some hard-nosed business creature with a rhinowhip and silver lamé shoulder-pads who boots her busy bee out of the door at dawn each day with the stern injunction, *Go and make honey*!

~

Mrs Troll – who knows all and sees all – said that my financial services advisor's nephew, pie-shy-guy Perci-Preece, went to Gran Canaria and got beaten up outside a nightclub by Mexicans. I puzzled over this for ages – until the penny dropped that she meant Moroccans.

August

To the Hotel Quirinale in Rome for our Silver Wedding Anniversary. It's not in any guide book, but it's where the characters stay in *Tender is the Night*. I doubt if it has been visited much since Fitzgerald's day – a ghostly bar, huge empty public rooms, dusty red velvet curtains, vast marble staircases. An atmosphere of faded opulence. Then by train to Orvieto, where I bought ceramic jugs and bowls I don't need and haven't room for. Tristan stayed at home in Bromyard with Amy Tortue, the Montmartre tap dancer. When we got back we found he'd lit garden flares in the bedroom – he thought they were ordinary candles. Having recently passed his driving test at the seventh attempt, he has already been in one (non-serious) crash and one (serious) near-miss.

~

Owing to the biblical floods and the prospective hike in the price of market garden produce, Cousin Looby went all the way to Asda to get "two packets of frozen peas." She had a bump in the lanes on the way back. The airbag went off, and the airbag broke. "My right tit came up all bruised," she said.

~

To Austria, where at the Stadttheatre in Gmunden a man played *Der Ring des Nibelungen* from start to finish on the tuba.

~

Chocolate Santas and Xmas Shortbread went on sale in Bromyard Co-op on August 28th.

September

I am a big fan of The Tenbury Tappers – nine old birds in fishnet stockings who tap dance to Nino Rota. It was hysterical – but no one laughed. The artistes were so solemn, with a lot of audible counting and sideways glancing to keep in time. Except in the "Springtime for Hitler" scene in *The Producers* I have never known an audience paralysed in such sheer incredulity before. But I'll say this – a fifteen-stone woman in the autumn of her years does not look good in a tutu. Parties for Sebastian Horsley, *The Oldie*, Paula Rego, Duckworth, Laura Thompson, the British Art Fair, and Malcolm Williamson (at Australia House). Didn't go to any of them. But we did go to see Mickey Rooney in Cheltenham – like finding out what Rigoletto is up to had he lived beyond Verdi's opera, though it was a miracle Mickey survived the night. He'd leave the stage now and again – I'm certain it was to plug himself into the alternating current to get his heart re-started. He is ninety-years old and reminisced at length about Lionel Barrymore as if people in this day and age might know who Lionel Barrymore was. He did an impersonation of Clark Gable that would have been bad even if people remembered who Clark Gable was. Film clips were played upside down and at random. When Judy Garland was mentioned he burst into tears, even though she died in 1969. Last week in Cheltenham they'd had *The Vagina Monologues*. On next week's bill was *Puppetry of the Penis*. There's a joke there if only I can think of it.

~

Also to Stratford to see *Twelfth Night*, with John Lithgow (my Blake Edwards) as Malvolio. "*Roger*! How great to *see* you!" he beamed, whilst walking away very fast in the opposite direction, exactly as Geoffrey Rush once did. John is very tall and was wearing a bobble hat, perhaps for a bet. He sent me a letter afterwards reiterating that it had indeed been great to see me. It was a shit production, with Viola played by a man and Sir Andrew and Sir Toby played by women. "Bring on The Tenbury Tappers!" I longed to shout. For there's an ensemble that could surely save the fortunes of the Royal Shakespeare Company. Nevertheless I'm interested in John Lithgow's playing my hero Anthony Burgess if I can get another biopic off the ground.

October

Oscar's eighteenth. He wanted lobster for his birthday meal – so I ordered a brace (is that the right word?) from Scotland. When the box arrived there was this scratching noise, and it transpired that these lobsters were still alive and full of beans. I didn't know whether to settle them in Miller's old basket and keep them as pets that'd need walking, or what. Well – I chucked them in a pot of boiling water and was quite the gourmet chef, i.e. I swore a lot and showed off. We were all over the place as a family this month – Oscar to Venice, Sébastien to Florida, Tristan to Paris (to see Amy Tortue), me to Austria for a few blissful days on my own. Anna was back and forth to the airport a hundred times.

~

I presented the prizes at Newbridge Comprehensive School, the former changing room for *Flick*. It turned out that my old geography teacher Allan Raybould M.A. is now the headmaster. The girl who won for one-hundred-per-cent attendance during her whole school career didn't show up to collect her book token, which was almost a definition of the word ironic. "*Fail*! She can't have it *now*!" I said. I asked for a glass of red wine at the buffet – an H.M. Bateman moment because only card-carrying poofters drink wine in South Wales. The metal-work teacher had to put on a disguise and run up the road to Oddbins. They gave me a bottle of Talisker Single Malt as a gift – which still had its security tag on. "You have very good shoplifters here," I said to the headmaster, whose smile grew a bit fixed. The alarms went off as we drove home past the Off Licence. Even I'd have seen the funny side if the VIP Guest Speaker at Newbridge Comprehensive School had ended up handcuffed in the cells of the Newbridge nick.

November

I hate travelling. Well, I hate *packing*. I never leave the house. I am a recluse, chiefly owing to poverty. Gyles Brandreth had to come all the way here when he wanted to see me, even if he did fit in a quick speech for the CBI whilst changing trains. So what in the name of Jesus H. Corbett was I doing in a torrid zone aboard the 9,570 ton MV *Spirit of Adventure*, quickly renamed *The Spirit of Dementia*, along with three-hundred-and-fifty paying passengers and my chums Craig Brown and Mavis Nicholson? Also at large were countless ants, horseflies, Rosie Boycott and television's much-loved Maureen Lipman.

The official reason is that I was standing in at short notice for Miles Kington, who was dying of pancreatic cancer, and also representing *The Oldie Magazine*, of which my cousin Jeremy is the deputy editor. Craig was in tow as Dame Beryl Bainbridge's stunt double – she backed out because she'd thought Brazil was near Boulogne and we'd go by car ferry. Co-starring in a rollicking drama that could be called *Carry On Up The Amazon*, if a Carry On film could ever have been directed by Luis Bunuel, however, was the real explanation for my presence. Everything that could possibly go wrong did. I'm not complaining, but I do feel I deserve the VC every bit as much as Private Beharry.

We'd been flown to the Caribbean, which was more overcast than Wales, which by Christ is saying something. Our luggage took so long to catch up with us, I expected to see a little chap on the side of the road opening his own branch of Next, stocked with my XXL blouses and Masonic apron. Captain David (as he called himself — but picture Kenneth Connor) kept making announcements very loudly and slowly and repetitively over the tannoy. You couldn't switch him off. He was always waking us up at dawn with another grovelling apology for alterations in the schedule. In the end I shoved wet towels down the speakers. Not that I did sleep for two weeks — what with the clanks, bangs and shudders, the anchor chain I'm convinced being situated on purpose directly under my bunk. And if it wasn't Captain David or the anchor it was D.J. Neil, the well-meaning Cruise Director (Jim Dale), summoning us to the Sirocco Lounge to muster for our excursions.

The ship couldn't easily dock at many of the little ports and jetties, so we'd have to slip and slide down the steps on to a tender. As most of the passengers were of an age to have been through the Blitz and the North Africa Campaign, peril was something they took in their stride. I had to be carried on and off by four Filipino stevedores, who considered themselves lucky my sedan chair had been left behind in the Herefordshire Balkans. Once ashore we went up a hill to see a rusty cannon, three goats and a bullock cart. At the turtle sanctuary I looked at dead turtles in a bucket. The sugar mill was closed — years ago. There was nothing to be seen through the windows, either. We had boys sawing planks pointed out to us and we went past hospitals, where the mortuary doors were wide open. Many of the museums we were taken to see were shut — except for an anthropological institute in Georgetown, Guyana, which had a terrible wax model of a tribeswoman with huge brown nipples. Craig had to buy me a drink in the bar next door that sold bananas and mild warm beer before I could recover. I nearly had a psychic fit and regressed back to puberty when I saw the bottled worms. The last British writer to visit the museum was Evelyn Waugh in 1933. He said it contained "some faded photographs and the worst stuffed animals I have seen anywhere." No changes there then.

Nevertheless, I could now pass a stiff exam on nutmegs and tapioca. We were shown every blessed branch, twig and seed pod. I quite liked the rum distillery. Bundles of sugar cane were crushed to produce a trickle of filthy liquid, which passed along a sort of drain or pipe into a vat of grey effluvium. We had a taste later — at 84.5 percent it was too strong for the tiniest sip. Chuck fruit juice on it, however, and you have Planter's Punch. I became happily hooked, leading to an onboard personal bar bill of £926.44. The drink came piled high with pineapple chunks and paper parasols — Maureen tastefully decorated her cabin with her collection of little umbrellas.

We had a bit of a run-in with the Maitre d' on the first night. He wouldn't let us go into the restaurant because we were "only the lecturers." In a way, I can understand his disdain, for aboard the ship was a little band of ornithologists, archaeologists, and sundry prattish professors who spend months at a time giving talks on cruises, on such topics as "How To Take Better Photographs" or "Flower Arranging at the Castle of Mey". One of these people (Kenneth Williams to the absolute life), a Humpty Dumpty big-head who seemed to me at least half-way intelligent enough to present himself as more intelligent than he actually was, kept videoing himself and broadcasting from the bridge, as if pretending to be a *News at Ten* correspondent. He told me that his website was the most visited in the world. "What?" I said, "More hits even than websites about blowjobs and big boobs?" I further and deliberately got into his bad books by asking what time he'd be amusing the passengers with novelty balloon tricks and napkin-folding demonstrations, as I wanted to book my seat.

Anyway, though we didn't want to be associated with that lot, we were cowed and pathetic, ready to slink away to the self-service buffet, or maybe to the crew's canteen for a mug of builders' tea. Television's Maureen, however, was outraged ("I've never given a lecture in my life!"), marched off and got it sorted out. It took an actress, with her combination of imperiousness and charm. The only problem was, the Maitre'd (a menacing Bulgarian – a variation on Bernard Bresslaw as Bunghit Din) was so smitten, he kept trying to cop off with her. I must say, Maureen took it very well. Escorted to our table like royalty, she wore ever more elaborate necklaces and green peacock feather head-dresses. She was Carmen Miranda by the end. The Maitre d', by now utterly besotted, slipped her his mobile number and e-mail. She said she knew all about Bulgarians. She had a Bulgarian home help who watered the silk flowers for two years.

There was a huge sigh of disappointment when Captain David announced we wouldn't be landing at Devil's Island. That's the former penal colony Dustin Hoffman kept escaping from only to be recaptured time and again. He also got himself recaptured on purpose, so he obviously liked it there really – and I'd hoped to see if it would be a good place to put people with hoodies and Asbos. Time had been lost bunkering (re-fuelling) in the night, however, and the ship had to proceed full-steam towards Belem, at the mouth of the Amazon. Cheltenham Ladies' College-educated Rosie Boycott was incensed. It was as if she wanted to start a Revolution and it was the Sixties again. Here was opposition to overcome and petitions to be drawn up. I expected her and Mavis to storm the bridge, cutlasses clenched between their teeth. Captain David's sole concession was to have the (filthy) house wine served gratis at dinner. By the way – the food was great. No wonder the napkin folders and balloon artistes stay on all year. Scotch salmon and Aberdeen Angus beef, Gressingham duck, and rack of New Zealand lamb – no foreign or untrustworthy muck caught or obtained locally thank you very much.

Not stopping meant a few days at sea. What a strange social life develops. The watercolour class was popular. The woman who ran it (Joan Sims) was so bossy, with a harsh, hectoring voice, like Anne Widdecombe's ugly sister. "Now, ladies, who's got a dry cherry?" she asked innocently. I was thrown out for laughing. The next day – roses. "This one is completely all pink! Drop a blob of clean water in it and you'll have a lovely crisp frilly darker edge to your petal. Now, ladies, who's got a glistening petal?" I was thrown out again. Mavis and Maureen stuck with it and their daubs of fruit and flowers were in the exhibition. Put it this way – Renoir retains his position.

That evening to a packed house Craig and Maureen presented a cabaret based on literary parodies. Enid Blyton and Jilly Cooper spoofs – done with such élan you'd swear they'd rehearsed for months, rather than for ten minutes, when they discovered an intuitive professional rapport. I wasn't wearing my glasses, but I think Craig impersonated the Queen and Maureen did Harold Pinter – so convincingly I thought it was him, and looked around the Sirocco Lounge in fear. You realised with Maureen that she can only be completely relaxed with an audience in front of her, and she's in charge. The Joyce Grenfell sketches she did for us were very funny – and moving, if you can get over the notion of Joyce Grenfell as a variation of the Jewish momma from the British Telecom ads. (Parenthetically, how come Maureen is a CBE and Liz Smith isn't?)

Mavis later interviewed Rosie about organic farming,

the campaign to legalise cannabis, and what it was like being a woman and a top Fleet Street editor. It helps if you develop a hard, prickly, beaky, stabbing quality, she might have responded, or else you'd not survive. I wish Mavis had told the audience what she told me – that the WI love it when she gives talks on vibrators. The bestsellers are The Pocket Pleaser, The Rampant Rabbit, and The Reliant Robin. We then inadvertently wandered into Quiz Night, and received a rebuke for shouting out the (wrong) answers to such questions as what is the name of the family in *Bonanza*? (No – that's *The High Chaparral*.) Who first starred in *Phantom of the Opera*? ("Michael Crawford, understudying for –" and Mavis named the Humpty Dumpty big-headed Kenneth Williams lecturer none of us could stand, and won a prolonged laugh.)

By dint of swinging the ship around on its anchor and doing stuff with cross currents and tides that would have impressed Nelson, Captain David got us not only to Belem, but to Breves, Almerim, Alter do Chao, Santarem and Parintins. In the rainforest there are these elegant opera houses, built by the rubber barons, and we went to see the one at Manaus, a palace of shredded and patched velvet, gold leaf angels, chandeliers and marble, that was used as a location for Werner Herzog's *Fitzcarraldo*. It could be Paris, until you notice vultures perched in the palm trees and on the knotted telephone wires. I must say, I loved Amazonia, even if the river water is as thick with mud and Christ-knows-what as the Rhymney. We went on one of those

stumpy three-storey riverboats with painted wooden balus-
trades to fish unsuccessfully for piranhas. Along the bank
were absinthe-green iguanas. Long-tailed monkeys leapt
from branch to branch. Red macaws and yellow birds darted
in and out of their nests. Bands of pink dolphins appeared
here and there in water the colour of bluish congealed milk.
On land, Maureen was doing some shopping accompanied
by Clive, the cocktail pianist. From a distance they looked
like Joan Collins and one of her husbands, or Lady Penelope
and Parker. Maureen's much more beautiful in real life than
on television, which must be infuriating if you are chiefly
famous for appearing on television.

The womenfolk used to flirt like mad with Clive, saying
he looked like George Clooney. When he started to sing in
his fey way, however, I said he was more like Rosemary
Clooney. He gave snorkelling lessons in his spare time and
had thighs plated like an armadillo. He needed his strength,
too, to balance Maureen's bags and parcels. I doubt if there's
a bead necklace left now in South America – though in fairness, when it came to amassing indispensable ceramic turtles, a steel drum, parrot wall-plaques, decorated plates and
coconut shells, hammocks, model boats, stuffed piranhas,
and toucan-shaped salad tossers, I win. People laughed at
my mountain of souvenirs, but I'm sure only because they
were dead jealous.

Given that Captain David (as he freely confessed) and
The Spirit of Dementia had not been in such a remote spot
before, we have to give him lee-way for not knowing that

the fresh water supplies would run out. Perhaps it was the fault of Clive's private snorkelling lessons? But it was no joke at the time. In the suffocating heat you get to depend on two showers a day. Apparently the pressure from the hose-pipes on shore was too weak, and the river water couldn't be sucked into the tanks because it was too full of detritus to be filtered. The Filipino chambermaids put a litre bottle of mineral water in each of the cabins for the old folks' dentures. Amazingly, the old folk, who'd moan endlessly if the hot chocolate wasn't hot enough or if afternoon tea wasn't laid on in a mud hut, knuckled down to enjoy a resurgence of the Dunkirk spirit.

As we floated down the narrowing channel, the ship was mobbed by dozens of tiny dugout canoes. Hordes of smiling and chattering copper-coloured children came to greet us – not begging or selling things, just out of curiosity. And what a surreal sight it was for them – a massive white ship gliding past the little dwellings perched on stilts, each house decorated with neatly pegged out coloured laundry. Fighting cocks and pigs wandered on the banks. Thickets of mangrove and pathless jungle enclosed us on either side. Venomous flies and big bats mobbed the decks. The next day I had puncture wounds and blood on my forearms and remain convinced I was attacked by a vampire – though how even an enterprising bat could get through several locked doors cannot be explained. I more than likely fell on the wrong end of a cocktail umbrella.

Disappointingly, we couldn't often venture ashore as the

tenders' engines were clogged with weed. A local ferry was hired instead, and so I did get to walk through the forest and into a patch of foraging ants snapping their jaws. Then I met a cloud of hairy bees. Vultures hopping around a rubbish dump, pecking at melons and banana skins, eyed me up as luncheon potential ("Guys, we won't have to eat again all winter!" – or whatever the equivalent is in Portuguese.) I went into a church, where a jazz orchestra was practising. They played Jerusalem Latin-American style, and I sat there enchanted. I gave the conductor ten dollars, as did Mavis. We now fear we have bought them and own them. They'll turn up in Herefordshire and expect to stay forever.

The dignity of these poor people was humbling. It comes across in the photographs of their faces. But if you were an Amazonian Indian and you'd peered out at this gaggle of British going by, surely you'd have found it symbolic somehow of the destruction overtaking the glories of the place – as the hardwood virgin forests and eternal greenness go for patio furniture? Were the old folk moved by the dichotomy? I think so. They were a distinguished crowd on the whole. Lots of former ambassadors, governor-generals, consultant surgeons and lord lieutenants, with whom on-the-move Rosie preferred or anyway tried to eat her meals. One lady had helped invent the transistor radio. One man was an expert in Norfolk's medieval church records. Another was a GCHQ boffin who'd programmed twelve Hewlett Packard main-frame computers for the Falklands War. He still lives with his mother and spends £64,000 a year on cruises. He's off to look at elephants at Christmas and wears an anorak all the time for his eczema.

What I realised is how wealthy the over-sixties are – so I'm sorry to say this, but off with their fucking heads! Their mortgages have been paid off and the semi-detached in Guildford is now worth a million, which can be accessed with equity release schemes. Index-linked pensions and lump sums come in quicker than they can count. The death of a spouse or two brings in a nice life insurance payout. So long as they have their health (and a nurse was on board to advise about diuretics), spend, spend, spend seems to be the philosophy. They have all been to Antarctica and Alaska, to the Baltic and the Black Sea, and liked to try and out-do each

**The author and an unknown woman
carrying on up the Amazon**

other, ticking off the expensive hot spots.

But after a fortnight in the old folks' company I detected little caprices. One man had a particularly annoying, wittering wife – then I noticed he'd taken his hearing aid out and no doubt not for the first time. There was a lady in the computer room so bored she was doing her Tesco shopping online for when she returned home. A loony who because of her extensive ill-advised face lifts we nicknamed Gloria Swanson (if she sat down her wig fell off) went everywhere with a teddy bear. The teddy wore dark glasses, "because he's embarrassed to be seen out with her," said Craig. There was a doleful man who was always last in the bar late at night – his wife had run off with his best mate the week before to run a pub in Solihull. After talking to me, I feared he'd fling himself into the river to meet the electric eels. Instead he hooked up with a burly fellow from Staffordshire with an impenetrable accent and seemed to cheer up. Perhaps on returning to England they've now moved in together? A maisonette in Uttoxeter, and their weekends spent grooming showdogs. I think Mavis also gave him some Agony Aunt advice and told them where to purchase The Pocket Pleaser. I particularly cherished a splendid Ulsterman with a Santa Claus beard. "Are you going to the calypso steel band dance tonight?" I enquired. "No!" he said firmly, "I'm too grumpy!"

The worst thing about being old is the young. On board *The Spirit of Dementia* there was a group of brisk girls in yellow t-shirts in charge of the trips, quizzes, and games of hide & seek. They addressed us by our first names, told people to put their canvas sun hats on, and ordered us in hi-di-hi fashion to say hello to our guides. If you are treated like a backward child, that is what you'll quickly turn into, and it brings out the latent delinquent. When the old folk realised they had to collect numbered tickets for the tenders, ruddy heck didn't they break into a run, elbows jabbing. The eat-all-you-can buffets would disappear. I myself, a meek author and former Fellow at Oxford University and Kentucky Colonel, found myself back-answering and sulking. Craig was rightly furious and shouted indignantly when he was accused by one of the girls of cheating in a quiz. In truth it was me who had sneaked a glance at the next table – to see what Cliff Richard's first hit was. By the last day my conversation had run out and I had a twenty-minute discussion with Maureen about dishwasher programmes. She told me about the fairground strongman who put his dong in the crocodile's jaws, thumped it in the eye to get himself released, and asked for brave volunteers. "I'll have a go," said an old lady. "But please don't thump me so hard in the eye." I was so stupefied I thought it was a true story and nodded sagely.

It was a glimpse of hell, particularly the layout of the wing chairs with brass studs in the Sirocco Lounge. This was the atmosphere of a retirement home or the sheltered accommodation that is up ahead, waiting for all of us, with faux kindly nurses longing to pump us full of tranquillisers, wishing we'd disappear. (Wasn't Philip Larkin's symbol of death a ship? The North Ship, which was "rigged for a long journey"?) Well, we did disappear finally. They switched the air conditioning off on the last day and bundled us ashore at eight in the morning for a (delayed) flight at ten that night, a rubbish charter airline called XL.* The cleaners hadn't cleaned the plane, the wine and gin ran out just as the trolley reached our row, the toilets were out of order "because too many people have been using them," and the seats wouldn't recline. Behind us – wouldn't you know it? – was the Bernard Bresslaw Maitre d' who, with no reason now to pretend to be nice, glared at us menacingly.

One poor man went mad and tried to steal a packet of Pringles off the stewardess in desperation. Another OAP lost his temper and flung his cutlery on the floor. When the co-pilot dragged a canvas sack down the aisle I didn't bat an eyelid – obviously it contained a body. The old folks were finally revolting and it was better than any in-flight movie! Names were taken and armed police and growling dogs met the plane at Gatwick. Maureen helped Rosie get up one of her petitions. I rather fear that some of my shipmates are currently in Wormwood Scrubs with orange bags over their heads.

*Which in little over a year later went ignominiously bust.

2008

January

WHY DOES IT ALWAYS RAIN ON ME? Because by Christ it
does. I arrived late in Bad Ischl to find the power supply cut
off, the meat in the freezer quietly putrefying. Half-tight
from Chilean plonk on the plane, I caused quite a commo-
tion, banging on neighbours' doors. Mrs Hitler and her
numerous chums appeared, waving their arms and flapping
their aprons in an operatic display of concern and anxiety.
Each of them scurried off to telephone an electrician – so
soon my hall was densely crowded with electricians and
their mates from rival firms, strangers from upstairs gliding
on stage and carrying Christmas trees and brown paper
packages tied up with string, everybody shaking hands,
shaking heads, stamping the snow and slush off their boots,
expostulating and talking in German. It was like the cabin
scene in *A Night at the Opera*. All we needed was Harpo to
parp his horn and for Groucho to say, "And another six hard
boiled eggs!"

~

I was invited to the Bad Ischl Tattooists' Christmas party,

don't ask me why. It was held under the crystal chandeliers of the railway station restaurant. They were quite frightening lads at first sight, many of them so laden with multiple piercings they couldn't rise beyond an orangutan crouch. None spoke any approximation of English. After twelve or so drinks, however, I've always found I can join in the conversation in any language, though I'll thank you not to show me any video playback as evidence. *Yenta. Shmeer. Gevalt. Shlemiel. Meshuhanah.* Oy! To be fluent. But not even I'd have been so completely off my onion as to talk in Yiddish to Austrian hairy bikers. To give this story any point I'd have to say that the next morning I came to in a ditch with a swastika perfectly tattooed on my penis. Alas, when we got up from the table to leave and my companions said they were off to a nightclub, I made my excuses and scurried away into the snow and home, double-locking my doors.

~

The boys went off to London to see Cirque du Soleil – people dressed as green lizards bouncing on lengths of elastic. Or that was the plan. The train never left Great Malvern as "the driver doesn't know the way." This was news to me, as I'd always believed that trains stick rigidly to their tracks and that they are not normally renowned for taking wrong turns up lanes, reversing in fields, asking directions from clueless locals in their native huts. But Great Malvern in the January rain, eh? Or at any time and in all weathers. Stern cross-hatched gabled buildings, choked ponds and black privet hedges; wrought-iron wind-vanes and twisting chimneys – like a set design for a stage adaptation of *Dracula*. The few people shuffling about looked either furtive and guilty, or insane.

~

The attractive posh waitress in The Ptarmigan with the stockings and drawling voice – I just could not remember her name. Ashling Custard – Haddock – Pocock – Windsmeer – Grimjuice – Moonflower – or was it Flyspray? It's Cheeseman. Ashling Cheeseman. Her sister was in *Mary Poppins* at the Prince Edward Theatre. Verity Cheeseman.

~

Hoping to have my locks shorn, I saw a note in the window of the hairdressers in Bromyard: "Closed due to quietness."

~

Age Concern has introduced a Toe Nail Cutting Scheme in the Community Centre on Hoarwithy Road run by "our trained volunteers."

~

I was prevailed upon to go to a neighbour's New Years' drinks do, held so late in the month it might have been the 2009 one they were getting out of the way early. Rubbish as usual. When I think of the conversations I've had over the years about conservatory extensions. The nadir was when I talked to a retired egg farmer about migraine medication. I long for the courage to come out with Charles Gray's great line. Quite against his better judgment the fruity old character actor once allowed himself to be guest of honour at a dinner party. "Where do you find these boring cunts?" he eventually asked the host. "I'm buggering off home."

~

We went for a meal at a pub in Whitbourne, with the idiot name of Live & Let Live. Balmoral Salmon tasted of wet sheepdog, and if it had ever seen the River Dee I'm a Dutchman. None of the adjacent tables was ever cleared of debris. The staff hid in the kitchen gossiping. The waitress had three tattoos. "Actually I've got five," she said. The only things I could consume all night were brandy and ketchup.

~

Jeremy Beadle obit. Never trusting a bearded man, I always found Jeremy Beadle's high jinks sinister. He'd burn down your house or dig up the garden and then lurch into shot, ill-dressed as a traffic warden or a municipal park attendant, enjoying your discomfiture and compelling you to be "game for a laugh."

What I'd have enjoyed was if somebody had stamped on his windpipe. Why didn't go-ahead impresario Bill Kenwright put him on as Iago or (given his withered arm) Richard III, Shakespeare's practical jokers? Perhaps the answer here is that Beadle was not actually much of a draw with the public. A pantomime he was meant to be in sold eleven tickets. Beadle apparently once assisted a person with motor neurone disease to commit suicide – though surely the mercy killing should have been the other way round.

February

Ned Sherrin obit. Ned looked exactly like what he was, a big lumpy pumpkin-faced farmer, a camp haymaker. Was it old Ned who, when in the West Country once, asked a cab driver to take him to a club, and the driver said very slowly, "Thar baint be no bum in Wincanton?" I met him many times over the years, and I thought his way with anecdotes was dreadful and flat. I always felt I'd missed something. He trained as a barrister and seemed to think he was still oleaginously addressing the jury. Of a panel of speakers in Bristol a few years ago, chaired by Ned – Roger Bannister and I are the only ones left alive. It is like the plot of *The Sign of the Four*. The clergy running Ned's over-subscribed Memorial Service at St Paul's, Covent Garden, invited me along – but I didn't go. I feared the poisoned dart of an Andaman Islander, which is what did for Bartholomew Sholto on that fateful night in Pondicherry Lodge, in the classic Sherlock Holmes story.

~

Nobody wants to join me on the Severn Valley steam train for my birthday. Craig and Frances are in Scotland in a hotel "run by Russians" (so they say – what's that all about?) and the only other friend I fancy seeing is busy with lawyers, trying to obtain power-of-attorney for her sister who is in a lunatic asylum.

~

The Ledbury Rotarians are given a talk on "The Diabetic Foot."

~

Fawlty-ish goings-on in The Ptarmigan. In the background and in dumb show, Mine Host put on a thick padded snow-boarder's anorak, found a torch, ran up the stairs like a maniac, and I next saw him through the window running away quite some distance along the street. Yet the next minute – almost as if identical twins were involved – he was shimmering into the dining room, sombre and stately, performing his sommelier duties, showing me the bottle and doing the little performance with the cork, all without a single word of explanation. I was so stunned at his calm, I didn't like to make enquiries about the emergency.

~

After the Sung Eucharist complete with bongos, the vicar announced that he has Stage II breast cancer – a nice example of God's custard pies, as he's not even a woman vicar (or priestess as they should be called). Stress brought on by the compulsory installation of disabled toilets in the vestry will be at the back of it.

~

I had to call International Directory Enquiries for the President of Italy's telephone number (again don't ask me why). They put me through to a furniture shop.

~

Olive's Wool Shop is to close. When Anna bought a small piece of ribbon there last week for 48p, Olive said "You've doubled my takings." I said she should try making a living as a freelance journalist. Olive's Wool Shop must be the last place in England selling canvas whalebone corsets, cami-knickers and pink-bordered linen handkerchiefs. Olive has a habit or hobby of knitting colossal models of local VIPs, the carpenter, the district nurse, the mayor, the town crier, and so forth. There was something grotesque about these effigies, which lolled in her window. One imagined they'd spring to life on *Walpurgisnacht*, when according to legend witches meet on the eve of May 1st and hold revels with the Devil, crash through the glass, and start a killing spree. We'd only be saved when Peter Cushing rode to the rescue.

~

It's amazing what you find you can get used to. For reasons I'll not bore you with, because of a skin problem, for quite long stretches of time I have to go to the hospital, put on these black goggles, strip off, and stand in a sort of Tardis thing, where I'm bombarded with ultra-violet light. There must be more to what's going on than this because the nurses dive for cover. To get the ultra-violet rays working, I have to take these tablets called methoxypsoralen, which have the side effect of making the eyes hypersensitive to light – photophobia is the technical term. During treatment I have to keep seeing an eye doctor who is on the lookout for glaucoma. I haven't had glaucoma, but I did wake up one day and my orbs were redder than Christopher Lee's as Dracula. Duncan said when I told him this, "You always behave like Count Dracula who's convinced he's the bitten virgin. What's new?"

What does he mean? The man talks in riddles. Anyway, I was rushed off to the hospital and told I had bilateral uveitis – an inflammation inside the eyeballs. It went away in the end, but the trouble is the condition can recur at any moment, and eyes can hurt like hell because they are nearest to the brain, is Mavis' theory.

So picture the scene a few days ago. I'd been feeling a bit run down and my eyes were getting pink and scratchy. The pain built up and I couldn't sleep – and in the end I had to be carted off to A & E. Have you been to A & E in the middle of the night? It is full of drunks being patched up and nutters with six policemen sitting on top of them. I sat there for hours, whimpering alongside babies who'd fallen out of the cot, old men having heart attacks, and others perhaps just coming in to sit in the warm. Eventually an exhausted Asian doctor covered in blood gave me some eye-drops for what he thought was viral conjunctivitis and told me to come back the next day.

My ophthalmologist had a marvellous name – Dr Grope. Because he's German it is pronounced Groper. Nothing else was remotely as funny. I sat there in the waiting room with a man who'd squirted quick lime in his eye, another man who'd managed to get steel splinters in his eye, a woman whose head had swollen up to twice its size after an overdose, so her eyes had vanished to little dots, and a crash victim who virtually needed to hold his eyes in the palm of his hand so he wouldn't lose them. My left eye was now resembling a crimson pulsating grapefruit. I looked so alarming I was in with a chance to be Liza Minnelli's next husband.

Dr Grope poured yellow dye into the socket and clamped my head in a device not unfamiliar to Spanish Inquisition torturers. Lights and prongs and mirrors and goodness knows what else were pushed up against the eyeball. The official diagnosis – an ulcer in the cornea and secondary uveitis. I had to have ciprofloxacin antibiotic drops for the ulcer and another drug called cyclopentolate to paralyse the ciliary muscles, which enlarged the pupil and stopped it sticking to the iris, hence reducing some of the pain. Then there was a course of corticosteroids, to reduce the redness. All this lot to be administered every few hours, including during the night. I couldn't focus or judge distance. Reading and writing were out of the question. I tried typing – it came out in Polish or Hungarian. It was scary and I was nauseous.

Obeying to the letter a leaflet I was given forbidding me from swallowing my eye-drops and also keeping myself well away as instructed from the temptation to climb ladders and scaffolding or operate machinery, I had to go into the hospital every day for the clamp routine. As I don't drive, this meant riding on the country bus with the poor people, unmarried mothers on state benefits and bearded grannies off to market, and the like. Actually – as a self-employed writer I am one of the authentic poor people myself, come to think of it. I am your actual *mendicant*.

In a television hospital show or soap, it's all action,

drama, speed. Real life hospitals slow time up until it stops, perhaps even make it go backwards. The magazines on offer were so ancient, Michael Barrymore was still a beloved star and Ronnie Barker sold antiques in Chipping Norton. There I'd be for hours waiting around in a bare corridor with near-dead old folk having their cataracts looked at.

Well, I obviously recovered, didn't I – as when I type this it isn't coming out looking like the Budapest newsletter, *Új Magyarország*. But the big fear is that the eyes will go again at some point. Future complications might include fluid in the retina and an inflammation of the eye's blood vessels, which truly would muck everything up. Furthermore, the systemic steroids can have the awkward side-effect of reducing the body's ability to fight infection. I'm lucky I was prescribed eye-drops. In tougher cases, the eyeball has to be injected. If somebody comes at your eyeball with a needle, the last thing you can do is look away. Your instinct is to fight them off tooth and nail. Uveitis causes more loss of vision in the West than diabetes, but little really is known about its causes or incidence. If you are feeling ghoulish, google www.uveitis.net and think yourselves lucky yet again you are not me.

March

Joy is unconfined in Dewsbury as little Shannon is found, hiding under a bed with her wicked uncle – or stepfather – or brother – or whatever he is. Grandson? What a frightening load of people they are up in Yorkshire, feral. Everybody is related and interrelated, the women having had kiddies by loads of different fathers, the fathers not quite certain who their offspring might be, a complex web of biological families and step-families that would tax the brain of anthropologist Dian Fossey, the *Gorillas in the Mist* woman. (In fairness, toffs will be equally as inbred.) Out on the streets with their cans and fags and obesity – civilisation has passed these folk by. Mind you, I envy the riches they receive by way of state benefits. They are a privileged class. In many ways, I rather fancy being a single mother in Dewsbury, with the Department of Health and Social Security delivering wheelbarrows full of grants and maintenance allowances direct to the door every five minutes. Much preferable to my present snakes-and-ladders existence.

~

Depressed and drooping like a bowl of wilted tulips, I googled suicide – or what is these days euphemistically called self-deliverance. The instructions were in Dutch. What am I meant to do? Beat myself over the head with a clog?

~

Though it is everybody's dream to run away and join a circus, they never do. Rather than tinsel and spangles, people end up wearing nasty little charcoal grey suits, their lives circumscribed by retail banks and cost accountants and accidental disability and death insurance policy premiums. My own children inevitably pick up on my disaffection with the cold-hearted New Puritan ethos, with its imposition of rules and norms, but perhaps they have taken it too far. Tristan particularly early on decided to be a misfit and failed exams through the brilliant expedient of not turning up for them. He did art for three years in Hereford and never produced a single picture, drawing or sculpture – in one way as I'm always saying a proud Dadaist statement, in another proof he was a lazy directionless sod. I suppose it was quite a worry really. He was finding his own way of heading for middle class inertia and unhappiness. Teachers and lecturers were always phoning me up complaining – I was only semi-sympathetic, as regarding tests and certificates, where did Magdalen College, Oxford, ever get me, eh? But the moment did come when I wanted his room for my collection of Sylvac Face Pots, so I changed the locks. Tristan worked for a season as a cocktail waiter on a Provençal barge. He was a tour guide at Mont St-Michel, inventing his spiel and telling the visitors that it was originally built for witches. He then spent a day last month with his godfather Mark Rylance, who suggested circus school.

It was an inspired idea. I wish I'd thought of it. I love circuses and had taken Tristan when in his pushchair to the one in Budapest – seals playing trumpets and bongos, brown bears riding ponies, parades of elephants and stallions rearing up on their hind legs. Of course you don't get animal acts anymore, but the acrobatics are much more thrilling, with people flying between the earth and sky, the spotlights picking out their lovely figures. You can't beat the charged atmosphere, the red velvet curtains – the vitality.

The Academy of Circus Arts sends you out on the

road for six months under the Big Top. One week Windsor, the next Wallasey, the next Horsham, then Carlisle... An enormous amount of endurance is required, as the students zigzag the country, literally learning the ropes, erecting and dismantling the Big Top in all weathers. We sent off an audition DVD of Tristan acting the giddy-goat – miraculously this was accepted and he has now been waved off to the headquarters of Zippos Circus, near Newbury.

The Academy was founded by Zippo himself, Martin Burton, in 1992. Martin's little yellow clown car is stored in the circus warehouse near Newbury, not used in any case because the doors won't fall off. Martin is eminent don Christopher Ricks' son-in-law and I can't help wondering if Professor Ricks is these days really in the ring as Professor Popcorn, assisted by George Steiner in baggy-pants and John Bayley brandishing a soda siphon. I put this to Martin. "Could be," he said. "Academics are all mad."

Martin once put himself in hospital when his fire-eating went wrong (he sucked when he should have blown) and now spends much of his time filling in risk assessment forms about what the chances are of Norman Barrett's budgies pecking the audience to death. It is also his task to do battle with the world's real clowns, the ones who work for local councils – e.g. the director of regulatory services at Birmingham City Council, who citing the Licensing Act 2003 has banned the Zippos clowns from sounding three notes on an exploding tuba, as this "would need to be clas-

sified as a live music performance and require a licence."
The cost would be in the region of a thousand pounds for
every site Zippos visits. Also suspect is the tightrope walker's skips – does it constitute a dance?

We made our first visit after a fortnight. After that I
couldn't keep away and was a fixture in the clowns' caravans. I loved the innocence of the entertainment. A magician folded balloons into Viking helmets and swords, flowers and swans. A Hot Hula Hoop Chick with tremendous
abs even got a hoop spinning around her top-knot. There
were wire-walkers, trick cyclists, and a clown called Little
Lou, who did gags with a ladder. Tristan carried on the ladder, helped the magician with his cabinets, and vaulted over
a box dressed as a lion.

~

Easter Sunday at Anna's family's. Her loud shrieking domineering parakeet of a cousin got on my nerves and I nearly
had to walk out of the house. I have nothing to say when
people go on and on about football, about which I know
nothing. Stella knows about nothing else. Bobby Charlton
and Stanley Matthews are the only names I can remember,
the one because of his comb-over and the other for his
comical shorts. I felt angrily cut off from everyone back in
my schooldays because I was bored sick by sport – and I
don't like any reminder of those unworthy emotions of
inferiority, shame and guilt. My attempts to turn the conversation round to bullfighting as I always do went nowhere.
Cojones, *Cuadrilla*, *Estocada*, *Fuengirola*, *Torremolinos*,

Generalissimo Franco, and the rest of the highly technical bollocks.

~

Thank God everyone has gone. Anna is in Bad Ischl with Oscar and The Shivster (as Siobhan his bird is called to her annoyance). Tristan is on the road with his Picasso Rose Period troupe of *saltimbanques*. Sébastien took the bus to his bird's gaff Pickles Palace and hasn't been seen since. He is to help Hope Pickles muck out her pony. I more or less stayed in bed for three days and read Carl Rollyson's *Biography: A User's Guide*, with its chapter on me and my hero Anthony Burgess; Susan Hill's *In the Springtime of the Year*, about in so far as I could gather a tree that falls over; John Bayley's *The Red Hat*, which made me wonder how much of Dame Iris's gibberish he co-authored; my old pen-pal Guy Davenport's first-rate *A Balthus Notebook*; *The Complete Frankie Howerd* by Robert Ross; a book on camp introduced by George Melly; *Hughie and Paula: The Tangled Lives of Hughie Greene and Paula Yates* by Christopher Green; *The Boys*, a biography of Michael MacLiammoir and Hilton Edwards, author forgotten — I recently saw them in *Filming Othello* on YouTube. I also watched *Jour de Fête*, *Carry On Girls*, a video from 1976 called *The Magic of Tommy Cooper*, and *Volunteers*, with Tom Hanks and John Candy. Tom Hanks was almost handsome when he was younger, but it is the blissful John Candy's film. Particularly hysterical is when he falls in the tiger trap and succumbs to Communist brainwashing. I received *The Spectator*, with a piece in it by me on Norman Mailer. I wrote a piece for the *Mail on Sunday* about the culture of the seventies. Made notes on Julie Andrews' autobiography for a *Daily Express* review and scribbled a few pages for my own comedy book, *Growing Up with Comedians*, Part One of *The Kill Fees Trilogy*. I left the house just once – to buy wine and whisky. I fed myself on oven chips and shuffled about like Badger in *The Wind in the Willows*. But the point is – look how much work gets done without the family about. Another night and day are added to the day. Who knows, if I could live like this all the time I'd be another flaming comet like A.N. Wilson or, if I'd afforded nannies, Allison Pearson. I could be a contender. I could have been Philip Hensher. He's everywhere, him, like shit in a field.

~

A couple in Elmsdale Road have been left "in a state of shock" after a plastic swan "worth around £15" was stolen from their garden.

~

Paul Bailey phoned to say he'd gone over to Rome on Easter Sunday in the Oxford Oratory. He has taken the baptismal or confirmation name of Ailred, as in St. Ailred of Rievaulx, author of the riveting *Speculum Caritatis* and *De Spirituali Amicitia*. He then told me a joke about a Chinese private detective who was hired to spy on an adulterous couple in a hotel: "They go to room three – I watch by climbing tree – he play with she – she play with he – I play with me – I fall from tree – therefore no fee." That's Paul all over.

Pre-Vatican II Catholicism one minute, mutual masturbation gags the next.

~

I asked Mrs Troll how Muriel was. "Terrible." Muriel has had three kinds of cancer, is on £50 a week and Garth is in the glue factory. But Mrs Troll didn't mean any of that. "She's heard I'm going to Iceland for the beaches and the dolphins and wants to come with me."

~

These photographs in the papers of children with cleft palates. I don't know what precisely is being bought or offered for sale, or what is being collected and on behalf of whom, but I'm so used to these eaten-away pictures by now, that when the other day I opened a magazine and saw a picture of a beaming and intact baby, I recoiled with utter horror.

~

Oscar asks about pre-decimal currency – half-crowns, shillings, ten bob notes. I felt my childhood had taken place in an era of stage coaches, women in bustles, Sherlock Holmes and gas lighting. But it was the sixties.

~

Kunz, our octogenarian Austrian friend: nothing he says about himself adds up. His address doesn't seem to exist. Nobody knows his surname. He told me once in a mournful voice that his wife was dead. Then on another occasion he said he'd never been married. He ran a cinema in Bad Aussee and met Stewart Granger. He was a businessman in Salzburg and had something to do with cable cars. He came to a fancy dress party we also attended dressed in a red mask, a top hat and a black cloak that was embroidered or embossed with spiders and frogs, like the character-baritone in *Der Graf von Luxemburg* – which as it happens was written by Léhar in Bad Ischl, perhaps with Kunz in mind.

～

Received a paperback of Byron Rogers' R.S. Thomas biography, *The Man Who Went into the West*. Two quotes on the cover. "A biography touched by genius," Craig Brown, *Mail on Sunday*. "Brilliant and unique... A masterpiece," *Daily Express*. Why was Craig mentioned by name and yet my own words of praise are left unattributed? Is it because nobody knows who I am and I don't count? Frankly, yes, said Graham Coster, the Aurum editorial director, when I enquired. Cheers, Graham! Adding to the humiliation – both Craig and Byron are much-loved chums. Byron always refers to me as The Beast of Bedwas. But hear this – when I start running amok with a machine gun in a primary school, it'll be because of the slow and steady continental shelf-like build up over many years of little slights such as this one.

～

Byron, who calls in to use my toilet free when skating between his nice homes in Carmarthen and Towcester, once told me that the reason he'd very sensibly never been in the least bit inclined to attend any orgy was because, "There's always a nude fat man standing on the stairs eating a ham salad." He was assured of this comical and off-putting vignette by an ex-colleague on the *Daily Telegraph*, who went to orgies in Golders Green on a regular basis. I don't think it was me that was conceivably caught sight of – apart from going to Golders Green to see Peter Sellers' plaque at the crematorium, I've honest to God never been near the place.

~

Craig and I vie for *Crossroads* memorabilia on e-bay – Roger Tonge's wheelchair, a set of Noel Gordon's sherry schooners, postcard-sized autographed portraits of the cast that once proudly adorned the foyer of the Chateau Impney Hotel, Droitwich. What with one thing and another I looked up Ann George on YouTube. There's a sequence from c. 1987 lasting 3.27 minutes and viewed 5,787 times (700 times by me, 87 times I wonder by Craig ?) where Amy Turtle is welcomed back to the motel. Terence Rigby frowns, half-smiles and huffs and puffs. The rest of the cast crash into each other as they try and enter the cramped scene, sit down, get a drink, stand up, go away, come back. In the midst of this activity Ann George/Amy Turtle has longish speeches, every phrase or word of which is garbled and given a star-tling random emphasis. It is likely that, though muttering indistinguishably she is also speaking in purest Black Country, where calling a *she* a *he* is acceptable locally – "Mrs Mortimer, heart of gold, he." Of course because it is *Crossroads* people will scoff – but had this been an extract from Ionesco directed by Peter Brook at his Théatre des Bouffes du Nord place it would be deemed masterful.

In relation to the chairs and occasional tables round

about, and in particular when she comes into view at about the level of Terence Rigby's knees, Ann George, the Dame Peggy Ashcroft of the Midlands, shows herself to be about two-foot tall, perhaps an inch or so more. I have ascertained through advanced doctoral research that the actress moved into a static caravan in Stourport-on-Severn because she said her house in Smethwick was haunted, though she never said by whom.

Once you get sucked into YouTube, though ... It's Alice's rabbit hole or the wardrobe into Narnia. I was up for hours in the night watching such highlights as Noele Gordon's funeral. She and her lesbian hair are buried in Ross-on-Wye – next to Dennis Potter. Was the coffin piped down the aisle to Tony Hatch's *Crossroads* theme music? Ideally her coffin should have clumsily criss-crossed with another coffin at a central aisle meeting-point, in homage to the classic closing credits.

~

Staying at The Royal Society of Medicine, in Wimpole Street, I read myself off to sleep with *A Colour Atlas of Venereology*. What kind of persons are they who give their life to compiling the official history of the genital wart?

~

Things have got so bad, I made an application to The Royal Literary Fund. They turned me down – and my cousin Jeremy is on the fucking committee ! So there we are. I am officially non-viable as an author and not worth the candle of propping up. I'd try prostitution, but I'd starve to death.

The alternatives that currently present themselves are murder, arson, assault, bombing and blackmail. Or else I could fling myself off a precipice in Bwlch Glas, like the chief constable of Manchester. Apparently the texts he sent in extremis were so garbled, his wives and mistresses thought he was communicating in Welsh. I'll bet you won't be able to move on Snowdon soon for people topping themselves.

April

Anna took a punnet of strawberries into work for her birthday. It was immediately snatched away by the health and safety police – one must picture them in body armour and shouting through loud-hailers – who insisted that the fruit had to be washed by masked and gowned qualified personnel behind closed doors in a designated kitchen area. What would these clowns do if she sauntered in with a nuclear bomb? Despite the baton charge and sterilising procedures worthy of Porton Down, none of this helped. When people bit into the strawberries, they got a mouthful of wiggly worms. Well, anyway Anna said she did. Another thing grown-up professional persons with university qualifications are not allowed to do in her office is boil a kettle unaided.

~

Gyles phones me from a taxi in Wales. He is doing an outside broadcast piece for *The One Show* from the housing estate where they make *Doctor Who*. "What a lot you had to overcome !" he said, presumably referring to Cardiff and its environs and meaning to be kind. But I've not overcome any of it – I am never allowed to forget that my father was a village butcher and I went to a South Welsh comprehensive and that my rightful place is in the shit. Otherwise I'd be on the jacket of distinguished Aurum paperbacks. Though I love Gyles like a brother (a figure of speech – as I haven't seen or spoken to my brothers since 2003), under the cover of his extreme good nature, what is going on? *The Dark Side of Gyles Brandreth*. There's a book that won't get written.

〜

Watching the fledgling barn owl chicks on the *Springwatch* webcam during my insomniacal hours, I suddenly realised whom they reminded me of – the Yorks' girls, Princess Eugenie and Princess Beatrice. The unblinking shiny round staring dark eyes are identical.

〜

Alan Coren leaves £3,173,948 net, according to the *Times*. I know he was industrious – all those rather facile humorous columns; all those appearances on *Call My Bluff* – but how in the name of Satan's Portion could his earnings possibly have added up to that? His collected trivia as published by Jeremy Robson won't account for it. He must have been involved with organised crime. This in the same week that I receive a royalty cheque from Random House for £25.30.

〜

Oscar is going to have to work at Buggle & Sons for ever, because we get ten percent off everything. Tinned peas, out-of-date confectionary, fireguards, toasting forks, bedding plants, pet food, slug killer and garden lime, i.e. the staples of a market town. Buggle & Sons also have a sideline in coffins – and if there's a shortage of dead people, they make rabbit hatches instead. The shape is indeed similar, now I come to think of it. Oscar heard about a very plain former shop assistant with a totally featureless face, like a pink scrubbed potato. They called her The Female Shrek – she's married to a cold-storage warehouseman and moved to Abergavenny. The Female Shrek was conscientious to a degree and also mean-spirited, as is the way with plain people when given a bit of power. She introduced a rule whereby the till assistants had to write down what loose change was in their pockets before they clocked on. Oscar said he'd have put 6p, 4p – piss-taking small amounts. The Female Shrek notoriously declared £86.

~

At Worcester Crown Court a farmer is convicted "for having sex with a cow," is refused bail, and is warned he'll face a long prison term. I know they are flirtatious, those Friesians, but what kind of world do we live in, eh? Duncan said that the first thing he was taught at the £5,825 a term St Paul's was don't have sex with cows because *they'll suck you in*. Sage advice.

~

I had a sharp shooting pain in my right bollock. Oh here it comes at last, I thought – cancer of the scrotum or the prostate starting to squeak. It turns out that because I'm so fat, my thighs are crushing my testicles when I lie down. So

here's another new career horizon opening up – to sing the
role of Ruth in *The Pirates of Penzance*, and the other prin-
cipal contralto G & S parts, Katisha, Queen of the Fairies,
Poor Little Buttercup. I could make a belated living as an
ingénue.

~

Being fat, I have fat people's ailments. We were in London
for Trevor Nunn's musical of *Gone With the Wind* – which
wouldn't have been so bad if only they'd cut the songs – and
I started to have this cramping pain across the top of my
Space Hopper of a belly. Now and again there were agonis-
ing spasms right round my chest and shoulder blades, like
the tightening hoop of angina. It was a hiatus hernia. My
stomach was being forced up into the thorax and beyond –
and basically I was turning myself inside out, like one of
those buildings with the pipes and electrical power conduits
trendily on view, the Pompidou Centre or Lloyd's. My lungs
were set to be dangling by my ears and I'd be wearing a truss
on my head. I couldn't sleep for the discomfort – several
times I had to try and sink into a hot bath or press myself
against cold bathroom tiles. The beauty of it was, we were
staying again at the Royal Society of Medicine, and *could I
find a fucking aspirin*? There wasn't a spot of codeine, ibu-
profen or paracetemol to be had in the entire place. Not even
an illustrated edition of *The Differential Diagnosis of Yaws*
could distract me. Eventually I staggered off to the twenty-
four hours Tesco's in Marylebone High Street and bought
jumbo packs of Zantac, Nurofen, Gaviscon and Rennies. I

grabbed all I could off the shelves and stuffed pills and potions down my throat in front of the alarmed multi-cultural check-out girl. I forgot that Andrews Liver Salts needs water. When I was a child, Auntie Dolly, my grandfather's old nanny, used to make a thing of opening her canister of Andrews Liver Salts, spooning the powder carefully into a glass. It was like being present at the creation of witch's milk. With Andrews Liver Salts all over my face it looked like I was on a cocaine binge. Anyway, I'm not allowed to lie horizontally. I might as well be hooked on the back of the bedroom door at night from now on and left to swing gently from side to side.

May

To a wedding in Hampton Loade. Elderly former colleagues of Auntie Pawsey's from the oil rigs, their second or third time around, who'd met bell ringing. The service included the usual embarrassing flute and guitar serenade by well-meaning and statutorily incompetent relatives. At the reception, the lady caterer shouted out instructions about going up to the buffet. She was winningly aware of her sergeant-major parade ground style. "My husband says I've got the biggest mouth in Belbroughton," she boomed. You can see the Midlands human type that Shakespeare got Mistress Quickly from. As usual I was flanked by estate agents and retired nonentities. Loft conversion chatter and so forth. No wonder I hate going out.

~

I ran across a family we know from West Malling, Kent. Grossly pampered only-child little Lennon is actually in his teens, but as his mother likes to think of him still as six years of age, I always allege she keeps him in a box to stop him growing. This is how they maintained a supply of dwarves in Goya's Spain. His full-on pushy mother really does still cut up his food. We heard all about – my God we did – Lennon's prowess at cricket, football, drumming, and a thousand other supervised activities. Intermediate conversational Mandarin Chinese, advanced astrophysics, playing the lute and the Welsh harp. It took all my powers of persuasion to stop him from showing us his Marine bugle and sounding Taps. When in the round-the-clock timetable does he ever daydream I wonder? Has he kissed a girl yet or heard about wanking? Here's what'll happen – either Lennon will allow himself to carry on being smothered and oppressively over-parented and in middle age will still be at home, wearing a cardigan and staring at a computer screen, his back copies of *New Scientist* filed in chronological order and his mother still whimpering, "Is one Nobel Prize *so* much to ask from a child after all I've done?" Or else he'll appear one day soon with a shaven head, piercings and pronounced Goth tendencies. He'll have a Hell's Angel fiancée in a leather corset who drinks White Lightening. Her teeth will have been knocked out from bare-knuckle fighting and Lennon will be besotted. I'll have a good laugh when it's the latter scenario.

~

Mrs Troll is going to Iceland on a coach from Swansea.

Though the ferry departs from Newcastle, she's taking the bus to Glasgow first and will double back – because to change for Newcastle in Carlisle, the obvious thing to do, is more expensive. Her itinerary makes perfect sense to Mrs Troll, with her frugal Scottish blood. If she went to County Galway she'd probably go via Munich.

~

Fire crews from Ewyas Harold and Peterchurch attended a chimney fire and "took twenty minutes to put out the flames."

~

I receive an almost transcendentally boring postcard from the Queen Mother's flower arranger. He's in Corsica. "France is well over a hundred miles away and yet Italy is only fifty miles." I honestly don't know what I am conceivably meant to do with this information. It is like a translation exercise. "The farmer is working in the field." "The oranges are sold in the market." "Mine is a large plantation, would you like to work in it?" These from *Learn and Speak Swahili in Forty Days*. Or perhaps the Queen Mother's flower arranger is attempting to communicate with me in SIS code? "The porters will arrive tomorrow." "Plenty of water is available in the rivers during the monsoon."

~

I record a radio programme in The Rosie Boycott Memorial Pavilion at Hay-on-Wye, with its dodgy guy-ropes. What a hellish place, the landscape so green, nothing but green.

After a downpour – nothing but mud. It was like Flanders. All we needed were a few poppies, a shell burst and a mouth organ and it's *Journeys End*. Rosie Boycott much in evidence on the posters and in the leaflets – the Hay Queen – interviewing the likes of Jeremy Clarkson and Jamie Olivier and General Sir Peter de la Billiere DSO, without whom where would English literature be? Though I'd sent her messages that I'd be around, she never replied. She never thanked me adequately for the inscribed books I once sent to her and Charlie, either, so I wish I'd pushed her in the Amazon with the piranhas when I'd had the chance. I was however asked for my autograph by a Japanese woman – possibly the same Japanese woman, or from the same family, or her great-granddaughter, who'd asked for my autograph outside the Palladium years ago, when I was with Denis Quilley. I can't remember what nonsense I scribbled then or now, but it was something like *Yours Very Sincerely*, *Edward Everett Horton* or *My Best Regards*, *Claude Rains*.

June

Since being on a diet and on the wagon (save at weekends and evenings) I have been nothing but ill. There is a lesson here. But the Big Slim was becoming necessary. Such has been my girth, to reach the table or my keyboard I either need to grow my arms or scoop a large disc out of the wood. So I gave the heave-ho to cheese and chutney snacks and my beloved French red wine – and (applaud now) I have shed seventeen pounds in six weeks. Three more stones and

I'll be normal*. But I've been coughing and coughing. I go bright crimson, my nose bleeds and my bloodshot eyes nearly shoot out of my skull, as in a cartoon. The doctor has put me on antibiotics, which are doing nothing. Nobody had coughed this much since Greta Garbo as Camille. I've been coughing so much I sucked my trousers up my arse.

The coughing fits lead to choking. It wasn't so bad when a session culminated in a good old globule of phlegm, even if it was streaked with blood. But I've been producing industrial quantities of clear gleaming sticky mucus and (a new development) pink foam. I only feel not too terrible when standing up. Once when I blacked-out I knocked out a tooth, so the following Monday was spent in the care of an NHS fang bandit, as drills and blow torches got to work rebuilding my gnasher at a cost of £44.60. I then passed the worst night of my life – pretty continuously coughing and choking and making a frightening howling, rasping noise as

---

*It has piled back on, and with interest. I was recently (2009) mistaken at Venice Treviso Airport for Wayne Knight, the evil computer geek in *Jurassic Park* and Newman the mailman in *Seinfeld*. American backpackers wanted their photograph taken with me. Now I can't even go out of my door for fear of being mobbed because people are absolutely convinced I'm brass-lunged YouTube sensation Susan Boyle (b. 1961, but looks half-a-century older), who belted out Herbie's "I Dreamed a Dream" on *Britain's Got Fuck All Talent*. Susan, who has successfully managed never to be employed, is a church volunteer at Our Lady of Lourdes in West Lothian and who when not residing adjacent to The Roger Lewis Mentally Handicapped Publisher's Wing in The Priory still lives with her cat Pebbles in her late mother's council house.

I gasped for air. I was in the GP surgery at nine and given another full examination. Gallons of blood were taken and I was sent to hospital for a chest X-ray. The upshot – bronchial pneumonia.

Sleeping for more than twenty minutes at a time is impossible, as the lungs fill up and I start choking again. We tried putting the head of the bed up on six-inch wooden blocks, like the chocks for the Red Baron's Fokker DR9, but twice it collapsed in the night and Anna started screaming from the shock. Piles of pillows don't help for some reason.

I'm in the fourth week of this now. Two further courses of antibiotics – including big yellow bomber ones – have done nothing. The black-outs have occurred four or five times. I went over in the kitchen and smashed my arm on a chair. Luckily the ground broke my fall, as Spike Milligan used to say. But I am covered in bruises, like the victim of spousal abuse. The technical name for the black-outs is apnoea – the respiratory centre in the brainstem sends nerve impulses that regulate the contraction of the diaphragm and muscles in the chest wall, hence controlling the rate of breathing and, with the airways obstructed, over I go. This happened to Bush when he ate the pretzel.

Having reassured the pharmacist that I'm neither pregnant nor breast feeding, I've now been prescribed gastro-resistant tablets called Omeprazole, a proton pump inhibitor to reduce the production of acid in the stomach. The theory is that these acids from the hiatus hernia problem keep leaking into my lungs, setting off the infections and everything else. I should be dead really.

~

To Sébastien's squeeze Hope Pickles' house. Our first time there, so I was anxious to make a good impression. I think we can say I made a memorable impression. Trying to suppress a coughing fit, I only blacked-out, keeled over onto the carpet and put my head through the widescreen telly. *Rosemary's Baby* was on, and it looked like I'd decided to head-butt Ruth Gordon. Everybody laughed, assuming I was drunk. It has happened more than a few times since, the cycle of coughing and choking and collapsing – I collapsed backwards over the bed and landed on top of Anna at 3 a.m. That's not something that's otherwise been occurring for twenty years. Anyway, Sébastien was mortified.

~

To the Liversidges' new house near Ludlow for luncheon. We had to sit outside, and I'm not one for soft undulating views, with rabbits everywhere and the birds shouting at nothing. There was a stench of fish, like cat food. Dorothy Liversidge later said she had no sense of smell, which would explain it. But this was our meal – fish stew. Dorothy told us a good story about how her ninety-year-old mother had escaped the other day from her maximum security twilight home and spent the afternoon at the circus. It was the best time she'd had in years. What a magical little film this would make – this ninety-year-old lady running away to join a circus, appearing up on the tightrope with a parasol, and she totally fits in with the spangled acrobats and aerial-ists, is accepted by the circus folk, and she's no longer a sad old bat. I would cast Liz Smith.

~

For the eight years I have been contributing to a national tabloid I have been kept on the same modest fee, so I am already receiving less in real terms, and the freelance is right at the end of the queue, worse off than a Victorian child shoved up a chimney. A rumour reached me that as a reward for my loyalty and diligence, the humble fee was to be cut by twenty-five percent. I wrote in a panic to the editor, saying that a "rumour has reached me that some pusillanimous middle-management fucking arse-creep is intent on cutting my already laughable fee by twenty-five percent…" And of course the editor wrote back by return saying, "That pusil-lanimous middle-management fucking arse-creep cutting your already laughable fee by twenty-five percent was me, so thanks for that." Oh fuck. This exchange will be taught in management training courses. But, as Kenneth Williams would say, it's a *disgrace*.

~

Hope Pickles' mother said that what she'd most aspire to is a house with "electric gates." Hope Pickles herself is now a waitress at a pub with a strict policy about children. Little cards were on each table – "Some parents are immune to the noise their children make. This sort of behaviour is not appreciated by the vast majority of our customers. We only have a limited supply of high chairs which must be pre-booked…" On and on the guidelines went. I abhor children as much as King Herod, but this sort of thing made me long to fill the place with exuberant delinquents brought by bus from every orphanage, bedlam and borstal I can find. Can you imagine the French or the Italians laying down shitty laws about children? It must be a Catholic thing, loving babies and children, enjoying their company even – whereas in the damp and Puritanical north, the young are there to be frowned at, considered as pests or evidence of sin.

~

We've been getting to know some of Tristan's new chums – a frowning Canadian with a psychology degree who wants to be a rock-and-roll juggler; a lugubrious Belgian Boy Scout who plans to be Bart the Clown; and a cheerful and voluble Scottish person called Tam with huge earrings and self-applied tattoos, who is perfecting a drumming act with kitchen utensils and rubber chickens. Ian and Jackie do a virtuoso dancing routine – but I sensed coldness in their clinches and I was right. They were a former item. By Wallasey they had a new dance, which choreographed their proud rejection, turning their back on each other, head held high. One of the heart-stopping stars is Miss Disa, from Spring Green, Wisconsin, who wears green leather boots and pink hot-pants and swings around on a rope. Tristan has moved into her caravan. So if the caravan is rocking, don't come knocking.

~

News reaches us from Abergavenny that The Female Shrek,

with her throbbing pink sugar mouse glow, has been and had a tattoo done, of her own personal design too – but no one in Wales or England has dared broach the subject of its whereabouts. Talking of tattoos, Oscar said he thinks he caught a glimpse of Kung Fu Panda when a Buggle colleague bent down to search for spare parts for a Goblin Teasmade.

~

A gardening club in Kington is "looking forward to receiving a new greenhouse thanks to a quiz night fundraiser."

~

To Magdalen College, Oxford, and the 550th Anniversary Garden Party. Hope Pickles didn't stop jabbering the whole journey about people whose names mean less than nothing to me. Ellie Walmington this, Ellie Walmington that. Ellie Walmington went to Saudi Arabia and came back her hair bleached blonde and now it's gone ginger. Abbi Yorke sees ghosts in her bedroom. Lulu Corbett has a phobia that sharks will be released in public swimming pools. On and on it went. We parked in Marston Road, next to what I can only describe as a mosque. (It was a mosque.) Had a picnic in the Fellows' Garden. Punts going by. The occasional orange plastic canoe. Some people's children were so badly behaved, I wished I'd had those pub guidelines to hand out. Throwing gravel at each other, brawling. I suppose it is only on the odd occasion like this that the traditional English middle class couple gets to be acquainted these days with its offspring and, without nannies and boarding school to impose disciplinary action, manners deteriorate alarmingly. Five hundred and fifty years – and Magdalen members do not age well. They start off well enough, the rugby players and boat club persons, each escorting a Pre-Raphaelite maiden. Within ten years, the paunch and thinning hair. Before long, the purple nose, the ill-fitting blazer and a novelty bow tie. By the end, it's panama hats and a plastic hip. The Shivster always manages to suffer. Her silver high heels hurt, so she took them off in Addison's Walk and trod in dog shit.

July
The Shivster says she was fourteen before she knew that tigers didn't lay eggs. I said that's nothing. Only the other day did I discover that Bob Marley had been a black man.

~

Under new laws recently introduced by the Department for Environment, Food and Rural Affairs, it will be a crime to kill a water vole. So here's something else to worry about.

~

Oscar bought a cocktail in Hereford, asked for a lemon slice to go with his ice, and a fat girl, cleaning and polishing further down the bar, piped up, "There's a shortage in Peru." Hereford – Peru. What an unexpected, surreal connection.

~

At a wedding reception in Wellington Heath, a forty-five-year-old woman bit the groom's ear off. According to the police report, Gaile Stevens "was acting bizarrely, dressed as a comical cleaning woman with rubber gloves and a broom. She ran off cackling into the woods and threatened to return later. When she came back, she beckoned Peter Lees for an embrace and sunk her teeth into his ear as he bent towards her." The missing ear has never been found. The Judge said, "We don't send mentally ill people to prison unless we can avoid it."

~

From Digbeth bus station to Stansted in the middle of the night. Mine was the only white face. I could have been in Tanganyika. So tired, so tense and on edge, I couldn't sleep or pee. The pain of trapped wind. Had I been able to give vent, the Ryanair flight to Salzburg would have shot far beyond the Milky Way, looping the loop as it went. On arrival in Bad Ischl I went in the rain with my orange umbrella straight to Zauner's for paprika soup. I'm here for a week of solitude to do some work.

~

I watched *Rebecca*, and I wish there was more of George Sanders' Jack Favell, stepping in through the window, always on the prowl: "I'm Rebecca's favourite cousin." What an unlikely and sado-masochistic marriage Olivier and Joan Fontaine seem to be undergoing – he's so bullying and irritated, she's so docile and nervous. They appear to keep separate suites in different and far-distant wings at Manderley, so there's not a hint of any sexual activity. (It hardly seems a Hitchcock film.) Maxim is extremely bad tempered and sulky – traits Olivier is always good at portraying. He was the master of petulance. The second Mrs De Winter is ill-at-ease and apologetic – she'd try anybody's patience, inviting them to strike her. We can't help but side with Mrs Danvers in finding her spineless and contemptible. The only character with life and energy is Rebecca – whom we never see, and who is dead.

~

Bought a pot of lavender for the balcony, which died. Two pairs of shoes and pink sandals for Anna, which didn't fit. Spent an hour hunting for my favourite propelling pencil. It was under the bed, where I'd looked a thousand times. Walked to the statue of the Kaiser Franz-Josef and the dead stag. Had a glass of beer and liver dumpling soup, which resembled a boiled brain tumour.

~

Later on, watched *Gregory's Girl*, which has an atmosphere of such sorcery – and there actually is a shot of a character reading *A Midsummer Night's Dream* in bed. Lots of odd, hocus-pocus little moments, such as the penguin wandering around the school. Gregory's brother being an expert pastry chef. The headmaster Chic Murray playing jazz piano. I remember Joe McGrath telling me a good story about Chic Murray. Chic was drunk and falling over on the pavement, but gave as his explanation, "I'm just trying to break a bar of chocolate in my back pocket." It must be a Scots thing, this whimsy – Andrew Lang's multi-coloured *Fairy Books*, Barrie and *Peter Pan*, and needless to say *Local Hero*, with the mermaid, the heavenly light shows, and the man ringing up the phone box at the end. The spell never worked for me. Four years in St Andrews and all it did was rain hard.

~

Walked to the Léhar Theatre and Anna called. Walked to the top of the Sirius Kogel and called Anna. As usual the ancient little old ladies, Mrs Hitler and her numerous chums, sped past me as I was dying and dishevelled and perspiring. Travelled back to England the next morning – you get to Stansted and it is a South American Latin Republic, full of dusky lazy-looking porters – a pervasive sullenness. Everything filthy. The Stansted Express was late. The Tube from Liverpool Street to Paddington had the hot breath of a tunnel in a diamond mine and was hardly a place for living human beings.

August

Talking about a place that's hissing hot, I'm just back from Madrid. Stuck in the Amazonian green damp of Herefordshire, I've been imaginatively in a dry Spanish groove or furrow for some months – reading a lot of Roy Campbell and Hemingway; and the film of *The Sun Also Rises* incidentally has the last authentically swaggering performance to be captured by a camera, Errol Flynn as the undischarged bankrupt Mike Campbell. (Did Hemingway name the character after his down-at-heel friend and rival, I wonder? Roy Campbell died in a car crash when returning from his Easter devotions in Seville and Toledo in 1957.) Errol Flynn is a peerless washed-up reprobate – Robin

Hood or Captain Blood gone to seed – and in his final film he nevertheless still retained a dangerous vitality. With it went an undercurrent of melancholy, as of revels about to be ended.

~

So off we go to Madrid by EasyJet. I really should move there permanently. I was enraptured by the mad nineteenth-century buildings and palaces, which look like the engines of infernal space ships. Oscar sent a card to The Shivster – and to get a postage stamp in the Palacio de Comunicaciones was to enter a brass and marble ballroom, with balconies and flights of stairs, most of it shuttered and semi-derelict, with bats and birds fluttering across. It is scaled for someone like a James Whale-era horror movie villain or Orson Welles, who of course did live in Madrid in the fifties and sixties, when he was making *Chimes at Midnight*, and I could see why. The city is flamboyant and theatrical, but actually not stagy or camp. There's a severe and ascetic quality to Spain – especially to its capital, which rises not from the sea or water but straight from the rocks. Now that General Franco's influence is fading, and they are having their equivalent of the sixties (Pedro Almodóvar movies, shopping malls), I do hope some bright spark doesn't persuade the town planners to rip out the onyx and stained glass Art Nouveau fixtures, get rid of the crystal chandeliers and dusty red curtains, and make the place spanking new. I fell in love with the Gran Café de Gijón, a graceful wood-paneled restaurant that has attracted the likes of me and Welles since 1888, and where I got drunk on Magno Solera Reserva Brandy de Jerez.

~

The Goyas in the Museo del Prado shut me up – that's what I'd aspire to be, a prose Francisco de Goya, if the Devil ever appeared in my lounge-room, offering to swap my immortal soul for something useful. What I realised about Picasso's *Guernica* in the Centro de Arte Reina Sofia is that it isn't a painting – it is a massive drawing, which imitates the black lines and smudged wet greys of newsprint.

~

We went to a bullfight at Las Ventas. Brought up in the slaughterhouse in Bedwas, blades and blood hold no fear for me – and it was fantastically exciting. We went behind the scenes beforehand to see the lots being drawn and the bulls assigned to the various matadors. We stood on gantries and narrow platforms above the holding pens, and these fierce creatures hastened from cage to cage. This must be the last chance left to experience something of the ancient Roman arena – it is hard to believe that it is still going on in the twenty-first century, when the budgies at Zippos Circus can't perform in public without an official licence signed in triplicate by the President of the Royal College of Veterinary Surgeons, perhaps indeed without the President of the Royal College of Veterinary Surgeons being actually there physically under the Big Top in the genuine flesh at every performance. The corrida is visceral, primitive, nightmarish – I was shouting encouragement and waving a white pink-bordered handkerchief from Olive's Wool Shop like the best of the aficionados. They are brave chaps, those matadors, standing there facing ten ton of angry bull – but their plight did remind me of my childhood, when I'd face ten ton of angry Mrs Troll, our beloved housekeeper, who charged around attacking, attacking, attacking, nostrils flaring. Though admittedly she brandished a wooden spoon and not a sword, I'd happily have plunged a banderillo in her ample flank, if such an implement had been to hand – which actually it was. When we went to the Costa del Sol in 1972 we attended a novillada in Torremolinos and took home a quiver of those barbed darts decorated with twirls of crepe paper as souvenirs. (How can someone only three-foot tall weigh ten ton? Physics is a mystery.)

~

There was a stall outside the Real Jardin Botanico selling Ektachrome postcards of "The Historic Houses of Chester." I sent one to Gyles, Chester being his former constituency. But then I suppose it is the case that in Ye Olde Print Shoppe in Bromyard, Norman stocks mezzotints of bullfights.

~

Returning to England and reacquainting myself with the Sunday newspapers – I am nauseated by the world in which I have to curry favour and eke out a living. Sir Isaiah Berlin at the end of his distinguished career concluded that "the longer I live the more passionately convinced I become that human relations are all in all." Which is to say that the pursuit or the possibility of human understanding and human toleration depends upon a fundamental sense of decency and consideration; that what counts is not being indifferent to the ills and predicaments of others. Well, it might have been civilised like that at All Souls, and good luck to them —but in the sphere of freelance journalism I'm treated more badly than a shit-shovelling slave in Ancient Greece or Rome. Editors and proprietors have a ruthlessness and a hardheartedness that has not room for anybody's happiness or pleasure.

~

"Circus people are different from other people," said Fellini. "They have a bond, and people who love the circus have a bond." When I announce that my eldest son is an apprentice clown with Zippos, where he is dressing up daily in striped stockings and perfecting pratfalls, I get one of two reactions. Most people remember going to circuses as children and mention the sawdust, pageantry and pomp with huge delight. Others put on a fixed smile and say what kind of life is it really, with these long-haired greasy gypsy louts and scallywags sitting in damp caravans under pylons. I find this insufferably snobbish — I go off them right away. Just as I always bridle if people use the word circus pejoratively, to mean *chaos* or *shallowness*. These are the insecure people, who need pathetic little traditional signs and symbols of alleged success to justify their non-existences, who cling to the company motor cars and pension pots, who are in thrall to sales figures and targets, the nine-till-five time-and-motion arsewipes who have

Stage IV cancer of the soul.

The worst reaction came from a horrible woman I met at one of these weddings I'm always having to go to – and I don't know how I stopped myself from punching her in the face. "When the circus comes to Newport Pagnell we have to lock-down the shops, otherwise everything would fly off the shelves," she explained, like it was still the Victorian era when actresses and showgirls were treated as prostitutes and actors could not belong to gentlemen's clubs, and circuses were a lower category again. When I said, "My son is in a circus that comes to Newport Pagnell," she didn't back down. An auntie of Tristan's from Clehonger gave as her pathetic excuse not to go and see him perform that she had to visit an exhibition of up-and-over garage doors. Another auntie reputedly said, "What's going on? *Our* family doesn't do this sort of thing! It is *shameful*." She had to be tactfully reminded that she herself had been born in a council house in Birmingham and was not of Romanoff blood.

As it happens the circus is a world of order and precision, or else people will die, crashing to the ground if the equipment is not rigorously maintained. Nor should the circus be the common metaphor for shabby glamour and improvised muddle – as the reality is dedicated artistry and poise. But yes – I wouldn't myself fancy living in the old bunker wagons, without running water or reliable electricity. I need a mint on the pillow. Though he hasn't seen a flush lavatory for months, Tristan nevertheless appears content. I know this because he doesn't phone or write.

When we turned up to see him in Finchley he was on top of the tent sorting out the chimney vents. He is now appearing in a few other knockabout acts, and the students' skills are evolving. One of the Hot Hula Hoop Chick's hoops spun off into the crowd and nearly took a toddler off with it down Regents' Park Road. One of the chaps did a dance inside a huge Slinky – like as if your washing machine pipes were coming to get you. High above the ring and without a safety net the girls were defying gravity and wrapping their legs and wrists in long strips of purple silk, making it look graceful and charming.

～

A man at the leisure pool in Ross-on-Wye jostled his way past a group of primary school children saying as he went, "Excuse me, paedophile coming through!" I thought this hugely funny – but of course the headteachers and local officials are up in arms, an emergency meeting of the Herefordshire Council's Cabinet was convened, and the swimming pool closed down.

～

Swivelling around to toss the empty Utterly Butterly packet in the bin, I fell off the chair. The next thing I knew I was crossed-legged on the tiles, like a pixie. A perfectly executed comic move, had I been Jacques Tati. As I'm not Jacques Tati, I was glad there were no witnesses – the children would have taken this as material evidence of my growing eligibility for ex-neighbour Garth's glue factory.

～

Suffering from insomnia, I watch *Lawrence of Arabia*. It is a fascinating story, which should be revisited by the likes of James MacAvoy or Cillian Murphy and done properly. Despite the burning dust and the pinks and yellows of the boiling sand, Sir David Lean's film is a cold film – Lean looked through the lens and worked his projector from such a distance, emotional as well as topographical, he might as well have been on the moon. The real Lawrence was a complex, histrionic creature, who simultaneously wanted fame and anonymity, and compulsively changed his name, to Airman Shaw and so forth. But Peter O'Toole is stupendously bad, well up to the standard of Sir Dirk's Von Ashenbach. He's like one of those vile, malicious leather queens that can be found to this day in Oxford and Cambridge Senior Common Rooms, and of course T.E. Lawrence was a Fellow of All Souls. O'Toole winces and grimaces, a gibbering death's head, his Lawrence only happy when he is filled with pain and suffering or when dressing up in Arabian costumes. I met O'Toole once, introduced to him by Jonathan Cecil – and I immediately recognised *the look*. He gazed at me with unmixed rancour, exactly like Lawrence when, having thwacked his camel and returned to base after rescuing that chap in the cracked salt flats, he is offered a slug of water by Omar Sharif. For some reason he takes this gesture as an insult, and so Omar Sharif gets given *the look*. Everything is a *challenge*.

Elsewhere in the picture – it's all men squaring up to each other, whether it is Jack Hawkins's General Allenby, chubby-cheeked Anthony Quayle's Colonel Brighton, or José Ferrer as the Turkish Bey. You expect Ferrer to get up from behind his desk and shuffle forwards with his boots on his knees, like Toulouse Lautrec. But Christ and a bear, to use an old Idaho expression, what a lot of bad acting is going on. Everybody could be a parody by Peter Sellers. Omar Sharif has Terry-Thomas's teeth. Anthony Quinn's nose is so hilarious, you can't take your eyes off it. He plays Auda Abu Tayi as Zorba the Greek. Let's face it, if Anthony Quinn was cast as the Reverend Collins in *Pride and Prejudice* he'd have played it as Zorba the Greek. Alec Guinness does Prince Feisal as a purring poofter, wafting around in his beautiful robes, chuckling to himself and glancing at people from under half-lidded eyes. The only performance that has any merit is the unimprovable and ironic Claude Rains as the diplomat, Mr Dryden. Exactly as if he'd dropped by from *Casablanca*, and in defiance of ten thousand hours of Sir David Lean's big skies and desert slide-show, Rains purrs, "On the whole, I wish I'd stayed in Tunbridge Wells."

September

Hope Pickles tells us that Ellie Walmington has had her hair cut in a bob and Abbi Yorke has discovered a floating bone in her finger. I found this out when we went to Compton Verney art gallery, where Oscar wanted to see the Kokoshkas. But we turned back because of the floods and went to Laylock's Garden Centre near Worcester instead. I love looking at gnomes, and bought two ornamental bird boxes. Garden Centres do represent grand days out for the old folk – one ancient lady was so bent double she was virtually peeping backwards through her own legs, like a circus contortionist. Hope Pickles told me she's never watched a black and white film, because they are presumably boring. I thought about this for a moment and it was easier to agree.

~

For two decades I've been waiting for the boys to grow up and go away – instead of which numbers are now doubled. The girlfriends are always here, needing to be fed, thronging the bathroom, taking refuge from their mothers, with whom they'll have fallen out. It's no joke staggering to the bog in the middle of the night, half-drunk and muttering, and some nymph shoots past – it's like I'm having hallucinations. I glance at myself in the mottled mirror and Leonard Rossiter grimaces back.

~

Autumn treats coming up in Bromyard – talks on "The History of the Spitfire," "The Stoats of Brockhampton Wood," "Acupuncture and Pelvic Pain," and "You and Your Radishes." I'm only sorry I missed the gala opening of Tantastic, the spray-tanning salon, as according to the local paper, "Teresa is very excited about her new venture and has specially decorated her tanning area and gone to a great deal of time and trouble to have it looking 'just right'."

~

To a wedding in the Lincolnshire mossy damp. Very evangelistic or whatever it is called – quite frighteningly patriarchal and misogynistic. I wish Rosie Boycott and Germaine Greer and the rest of the she-bears had been there to fling insults and rotten fruit. The vicar said it was the duty of the wife to submit to the husband, because he was a man and therefore head of the household, and hence obviously and automatically he would know what was going to be for the best in every circumstance. Patronising and retrograde – I thought this went out with Queen Victoria and the Brontes, the idea of women as chattels, defined by their subjugation to the old fella. The biblical sanction comes from Ephesians Chapter V, verses 21-33, if you want to look it up. This being 2008, I expected the bride to say, *Fuck you chum*, toss her bouquet into the waste bin, and storm out of the church with the best man for a weekend of riotous bareback sex in the Travelodge at Newark-on-Trent.

Then at the reception I noticed few couples in their thirties and forties; only single people dotted here and there, next to boring dribbling old great-uncles and aunties. This was because only genuinely married people were allowed in. And absolutely no gays. As usual I was placed next to dreary people who perked up when I explained how Corsica is a hundred miles from France, but only fifty miles from Italy! Then I started on ammonites.

~

The new neighbours from opposite were in Mahi's, the best restaurant in the Herefordshire Balkans, and an Indian one needless to say, and the woman talked to us for ages – but she made no sense. She kept going on about working in a box office and behind the bar at a theatre, as if we were already a party to this information. Finally she had to have it explained to her by her otherwise semi-mute bearded husband that we weren't who she thought we were and that here was a clear case of mistaken identity. Now it is bad enough to be so unmemorable that a neighbour who has seen us most days for six weeks can't distinguish us – but worse still was whom she'd thought we actually were. Suffice it to say Anna was mixed up with a local woman who could have been Hattie Jacques' stunt double and the man is a twenty-stone stroke victim who mutters out of the side of his mouth, like Popeye.

~

A man threw an apple at a passing Mazda MX-5 in Eign Street and then ducked behind a wall. "A number of apples were found by police officers at the scene afterwards."

~

You can't keep me away from the Big Top. I'm always taking along a Fortnum's hamper and after the show the circus folk sniff out the picnic and we get a party going. What characters they are. Tommaso Divincenzo is a contortionist who has positioned garden gnomes and cacti outside his caravan. Craig Attmore, a bit blobby when he arrived, has lost so much weight he can run up a vertical rope. The Ringmaster is Greg Milstein. Greg has travelled with circuses for a quarter-of-a-century. He was the first American artiste to join the Soviet State Circus – and in

Russia, circuses have the sort of status accorded here to the Royal Shakespeare Company or the National Theatre, the difference being that Sir Antony Sher and Dame Judi Dench don't have to build and dismantle the stage and auditorium every single week come rain or shine with their *bare hands*.

For six months now without a single full day off Tristan and his crew have trekked between weekend festivals, country fairs and seaside resorts. They hold plate-spinning workshops for the public, put up the posters, sell tickets, and maintain the lorries and latrines. For the first period of training they tried a variety of disciplines, from trampolines to clowning. There were group classes in dance, tumbling and balancing – and gradually they've been discovering their preferred skills and aptitudes. Jo Glover, a pretty Australian save for the bolt through her nose, developed a contortion table routine. It was tricky knowing which bit of this bendy babe was pointing at you. She looked like she could sing through a surprising orifice and still stay in tune. "You'll have arthritis when you are older," I warned. Tam Hewitt-Baker bought his rubber chickens. Tristan's official act is as Mr Twix. His face a chalky mask and dressed in old world clothes from Camden Market, he juggles billiard balls. Homage is being paid to the Jacques Tati and Buster Keaton films he'd always watched. His latest discovery is W.C. Fields, whom I am myself possibly a reincarnation of, because roses are not things that my life is a bed of.

October

I didn't have a pound coin to unchain a trolley at the Co-op, so I thought I'd cope with one of the gratis trolley contraptions they have for the wheelchair-users. I obviously made all-too convincing a cripple, as I pushed this cantilevered tubular chrome mechanical aid up and down the aisles – for people smiled at me indulgently and in a politically correct fashion. They even opened up a special checkout for me – and I had the wit, after I'd dumped the thing in the corral in the car park, to carry on limping and grimacing. When I got home Faye Dunaway was on the phone.

~

Has old Faye had a few spa treatments? To my untrained eye she seems to have at least got these new plastic teeth, which give her a kind of gum lift, stretching the skin above the upper lip, eradicating the rills and rivulets. "*Hey*, that light is kicking off my *face*!" she'd tell the cameraman, if she felt she was looking too ghoulish, even for South Wales, when she was co-starring with Oscar in *Flick*. I've been mugging up on Francis Bacon, in readiness for the exhibition at the Tate, so nothing scares me – but in *Flick*, when they sent me a promotional DVD the other day, I did find myself mesmerised by Faye's character's head. One-armed cop Lieutenant McKenzie's full lips and bright eyeballs seem to sit and eddy on the surface of her tight skin and to be worked independently by wires. Nothing dares sag.

Thirty years ago Faye thought my auntie Bette Davis looked grotesque – a portrait by Francis Bacon in fact – her cosmetic surgery, "a final scream against a fate over which no one has control: growing old." Every time Bette sat down her hat fell off. On *Friday Night With Jonathan Ross*, a chat show Faye endured sportingly to publicise *Flick*, she wore gauntlets that rotten cads might say were to hide her claws. I prefer to think she was about to dash off to her weekly falconry class, where merlins and kestrels swoop to her wrist. At nearly seventy, Faye is now the one who doesn't appear to want to yield to the ageing process – and I say good luck to her. When mad old bat Shirley MacLaine advised her to "give in to being old. Once you do, it's terribly liberating," Faye was appalled. "At some point I will do that, but I'm not ready to play those sorts of roles yet." Faye has a twinkling girlishness. She could hang out with Hope Pickles, Ellie Walmington and Lulu Corbett and not be out of place. She's not a faded star.

Howard and his producer Rik Hall found themselves adoring Faye for her prickliness and quiet hysteria, deciding that she was vulnerable and needed protection, the scarab-hard carapace something of an act, a defence against the Hollywood machine – and a defence against having to be on a planet with lesser mortals, as I saw it. If there was a brusqueness, a snappishness, a neurotic manner, it's because she is a star living permanently on her wits and nerve endings. Yet despite being Faye Dunaway, movie icon, she had no entourage during *Flick*. She dealt with it all on her own, returning to her Cardiff hotel on her own – though it had to be explained that her hotel of choice, the Dorchester, was

163

not within easy commuting distance of Pontypool. She likes the Dorchester because she is friendly with the Sultan of Brunei, one of whose relatives visited her on the set, and she gets a discounted rate.

The shoot was, shall we say, unto the last, eventful. I loved hearing about it. It was a good day if nothing worse happened than when the brake broke on the catering bus, sending it into a wall. Anna Karen was worried that she wasn't going to get paid, because her husband is in a wheelchair. She'd appear from her caravan wearing a white dressing gown and flicking fag ash. "Weren't you that little boy who came to see me in Rhyl?" she asked the director – Rhyl of course being where the classic *Holiday on the Buses* was made in 1973, two years before David Howard was born.

Because she's a heavy smoker, Anna couldn't hold her breath when she was meant to be dead, so they had to utilise a freeze-frame. Geoffrey Hughes, who played her husband, cheerfully spent three hours on the floor playing dead – and he wasn't even in the shot. Hughes, who now lives far from Wetherfield on the Isle of Wight, was a big hit in Pontypool, signing autographs as Eddie the Binman, even though he hasn't been in *Coronation Street* for twenty-nine years. Terence Rigby, however, as befits the character he portrayed, a thug called Creeper Martin, was taciturn. You could see why he was a favourite of Harold Pinter, as he had menace. He was also ill, though nobody knew, and dropped dead just the other day, after inviting Julia Foster to call in and see him in New York with her husband.

If a cloud of doom hung over Rigby, the atmosphere worsened on set. As it was Wales, many of the crew affected to speak the Welsh language on purpose, though reverting to English when your back was turned. This held things up, because they had to search for words – there being no new nouns in the tongue since the twelfth century. Then Howard's relationship with his cinematographer deteriorated. "Who do you think you are, fucking Fellini?" the cameraman and his team would mutter.

Post-production dragged on and on. I was keen to see at least a rough cut, but a big silence had descended. A screening planned for potential distributors last January in Wardour Street was abruptly cancelled. The rumour was that the negative was locked in the lab until processing bills were met, otherwise the bailiffs would be marching off with Faye Dunaway and turning her into guitar picks. When I tried to reach the director on the phone a sickly BT woman's voice came on the line to say "This number does not accept incoming calls."

I eventually received an e-mail saying, "I understand what depression is! The last few months have been Hell. Lost my house and car all in the name of this fucking film. Let's hope I don't end up like D.W. Griffith dying drunk in a rented hotel room. I'd settle for being Val Guest, especially if I could own a row of mews cottages in Belgravia." Like Ronnie Corbett in *Sorry!* Howard was back living with his mother near Llanbradach, where my father once had one of his butcher's shops. I remember a hatch in the floor, down which they'd winch sides of beef.

Then a few film festivals started showing an interest and it looked like *Flick* might at last be taken off the shelf. In Berlin £750 was offered for the Mongolia rights. In Brussels sci-fi fans in orange anoraks hoped in vain for Faye's autograph. Then The Sixteenth Raindance Film Festival in the West End planned a proper premiere, and so here I am in Cineworld, Leicester Square.

Ten minutes before the event was to take place, the projection equipment blew up. No red carpet could be found – and Faye needed a red carpet. In the end she made do with a stained old rug that would have embarrassed Albert Steptoe. Oscar and I couldn't find the right entrance and spent a fruitless hour going up and down escalators and through fire exits and into Great Windmill Street, Rupert Street and Coventry Street. We were joined by Hugh O'Conor, a nice-looking fellow in Donegal tweeds when out from under his Johnny Flick zombie make up. He was also lost.

Two hundred people were turned away, as the event was over-sold. The girl with the clipboard who was meant to greet invited guests was so inundated, she threw the list on the floor and ran off crying. Nobody knew what was going on. Duncan Fallowell took one look at Faye Dunaway, saw that he'd been upstaged, and slunk away to a gay bar in Soho. In fact he went to several. Hob and Knob wandered into *Brideshead Revisited* by mistake and wondered when the zombie was going to appear. Sir Michael Gambon is in it as

Lord Marchmain so they'd not have been totally disappointed. Faye, looking like she'd been beamed down from a distant planet, with blonde mermaid hair she could sit on, and a smile that reached behind her ears, and dressed fetchingly in a black cobweb, got stuck in the line for popcorn and was flustered to find she didn't have any loose change.

The bun fight was symbolic of the whole enterprise – zombies, post-industrial South Wales, bubble-gum-coloured comic books. I loved the film on the big screen, when at last it started. My name comes on at the end, which was worth waiting for. The movie crackles and fizzes with radioactivity. Because of the putrefied monster mask, O'Conor has to do a lot of acting with his eyes – and what an affecting actor he is, with a portfolio already of poisoners, sweet-natured priests and Jane Austen suitors to his credit. "That's our Hawtrey!" I shouted out – like Zero Mostel shouting "That's our Hitler!" in *The Producers*.

As for everybody else who has been involved along the way – Michelle Ryan, who played Creeper Martin's daughter, had her *Bionic Woman* series cancelled and she didn't manage to become Dr Who's next female companion; Faye is now in Warsaw trying to mount a biopic about Maria Callas; Rik Hall spent so long booking her flights he is fluent in Polish. I saw him talking Polish to a waiter in the Groucho and was impressed. If the royal family is wiped out and her son Ben Fogle becomes king, Julia Foster will be the next Queen Mother. David Howard went to St. Lucia, where he was bitten by a snake.

Mark Rothko's mighty claret-coloured canvases are like
Japanese meditation boards, a rarefied use of colour that is
very soothing. I don't normally enjoy galleries and exhibitions. I spend longer in the shop, buying Vermeer fridge
magnets and Francis Bacon fudge. But I was thrilled by the
cathedral space they'd given to Rothko at Tate Modern. It
needed candles and some Gregorian chanting. His pictures
work best when there are loads of them – oceans of purple
and orange and tangerine; huge spreading water meadows
of reds and blacks. One of the books I have here is a first
edition of *The Graphic Bible* by Lewis Browne (New York,
1928). The maps and charts were drawn by Marcus
Rothkowitz – and I have never seen the connection made
anywhere, but of course his big abstract pictures, too, are
cartographic. Rothko, whom Rothkowitz became, paints the
world as seen from above – the seas and mountains, forest
fringes and continental shelves. Even his jet black pictures
have hidden shades and shadow, which loom and shimmer
and have vertiginous geological depths. As John Buchan's
wife said of T.E. Lawrence, in a quote I found recently, so
may I describe Mark Rothko: "He is looking at the world as
God must look at it and a man cannot do that and live." Of
course Rothko slashed his wrists in his studio, dying in pools
of blood that resembled his own crimson art.

~

Oscar and I then had a splendid long luncheon in the restaurant at the top of Tate Modern, at a table overlooking the
river. We were there hours and later I carried on getting

drunk in the bar on the evening train back to Hereford. I didn't bother to find a seat – I just kept on lining up the Gilbey's miniatures on the counter, a queue of people forming behind me. From then on my memory is vague.

~

Pensioner Marguerite Hicks of Lower Bullingham, who because of her "mobility problems and a heart condition," has a disabled parking badge, was outraged to be sent a form by the Council's Equality and Diversity Manager, asking her to tick the box that best described her sexual orientation and religious beliefs. "I have never been asked that even by health care professionals," said great-grandmother Mrs Hicks.

~

One of my true regrets is that I never met Jennifer Paterson – though I suppose I did technically encounter her once, when I had luncheon at *The Spectator* during my younger years, where she was the cook. One of the other guests was Wendy Cope – or was it Posy Simmonds? Or Fleur Adcock? I seem to recall a mannish, cross person coming in and out anyway – presumably that was Jennifer. Though a devout Pre-Vatican II Catholic, because of her chain smoker's cough she always approached Mass in a holy terror of going into a spasm and choking to death, trying to swallow the wafer. Her nasty coughing if any foreign body touched her throat must have ruled out lots of things besides, though I've heard rumours that when making *Two Fat Ladies* she was liable to bang the cameramen's dinner gongs with abandon. Other sources say she was the last virgin left in northern Europe.

Those *Two Fat Ladies* shows are favourites of mine, though not entirely for the food. I enjoy the way Jennifer and Clarissa Dickson Wright waddle around Cornwall or Cirencester, always hovering on the brink of squabbling. They obviously couldn't stand each other, upstage each other shamelessly and tread maliciously on punch lines. The highlight is always when Jennifer has had one nip too many of the rum punch and starts singing, her bass deeper than soulster Isaac Hayes, who voiced Chef on *South Park*. Now and again, however, I do attempt to replicate a recipe – and for Halloween I made their pumpkin soup and partridges stuffed with apricots and rice. What an orange meal it was, right down to the label on the Glenmorangie bottle. The dining-room was decorated with an orange table cloth and orange napkins, stenciled with the silhouettes of witches. Hope Pickles came to the dinner and I lost her and everybody else's interest as I failed to describe the plot of Max Ophuls' *The Earrings of Madame De* coherently. I missed out a few final twists and ramifications and suddenly the narrative was all over the place. We'd got on to this because Sébastien had bought Hope Pickles some expensive earrings in Florida, which she mislaid on the school bus, but which were then later found by Lulu Corbett. Oscar said this saga sounded more like Max Ophuls than Max Ophuls.

~

I murmured to Beryl wasn't it sad about Pat Kavanagh and she embraced me for comfort or perhaps simply to remain vertical and said, "Yes, he was a great poet." Adding to the confusion was the fact that the son of Ted Kavanagh of *ITMA* fame was standing next to us, in the East India Club. Can you believe the web of confusing coincidences? Or does this sort of thing only happen to me? Beryl and I were papped later – so I'm looking out for a photograph in some diary of "Dame Bainbridge and Stratford Johns." I took myself to dine at Wilton's and ran up a bill of £187.

Pat Kavanagh's obituary coverage was so lavish one would have thought she was a head of state, not a London literary agent. It's like she was Benazir Bhutto. I said to Richard Ingrams that Sir Elton will be dusting off "Candle in the Wind" and a niche in the Abbey will have been booked. We've had front page news in the broadsheets; the nation plunged into mourning; Clive James*, Blake Morrison, Howard Jacobson and the rest of them wearing black armbands.

All this says rather a lot about the ghastly nature of our self-congratulatory, incestuous literary life. I never knew the woman nor know anything about her, but from what

---

*Quite one of the most revolting pieces of journalism since Clive James's Diana eulogy ("No, I never saw her again. Neither will anyone now. Not even once. Never even once again") has been Clive James's Pat Kavanagh eulogy ("On a grand occasion she had a way of looking unimpressed that could set the assembled company to wondering if they quite measured up"). It has become hard to discriminate between Clive's mouldy fudge and Craig's brilliant parodies of it.

I've been reading she sounded a total raving ratbag, as amenable as white concrete. She never made a single memorable remark – yet her very silence is being adduced by total fucking fools as proof of inscrutable genius. It would be more true to life if her perfect stillness actually represented just how unresponsive and bored she'd become after all the dreary adoration. Apparently, she was so diaphanous and grand, it was inconceivable that she'd be expected to travel by public transport, jostling with lesser mortals. The big unexplained mystery is why after having had her Sapphic fling with Jeanette Winterson *she went back to Julian Barnes.**

~

There is a small earthquake in Bromyard, measuring 3.6 on the Richter Scale. Because it is Bromyard, not only are there not many dead – not many people noticed. I thought a wheelie bin from The Ptarmigan had crashed into my wall. Several miles away in Pencombe crockery fell off a shelf, but didn't smash. Mr. George Webb of Bredenbury who according to the local press has "long taken an interest in geological matters" said it sounded like "two things rubbing together."

November
People still talk about the occasion years ago when The

---

*Kingsley Amis dedicated *Jake's Thing* (1978) to Pat Kavanagh. The novel is about impotence and rampant misogyny – with tirades about women's "exaggerated estimate of their own plausibility." How pleased was Pat to receive Amis's sweet offering, I wonder?

Female Shrek ticked off one of the new members of staff at Buggle & Sons for wearing coloured nail polish. When the same new member of staff cleaned the counter, she was ticked off again because The Female Shrek was "allergic to Mr. Muscle," which apparently lingers in the air "for three hours." If anyone messed with The Female Shrek she got her mother to come along and sort them out – it must've been like the manifestation of Grendel's mother in *Beowulf*. But at least Grendel's mother was on Grendel's side, not like the women in Wales. They eat their menfolk for breakfast. I always felt even our beloved housekeeper, Mrs Troll, who was almost like a mother to me, resented me, probably because we grew to be too alike and reminded each other of ourselves, though I don't wear a floral-patterned tabard pinafore. We both had forest fires inside our heads. And anyway it is not true that Mrs Troll always resented me – because when my books used to come out she'd sail into Waterstone's and put copies of my stuff on the bestsellers shelf, concealing glossy hardbacks by Danielle Steel and James Clavell.

~

My latest enthusiasm – Edward Bawden. Linocuts and neat little crayon drawings, book illustrations and careful pale watercolours of street scenes, principally pubs and shops and churches, markets and railway stations. His work is intensely, pitifully English – as in the poetry of Betjeman there is a love of customs and traditions which, though centuries old, are surely about to be obliterated, the agricultural machinery repairer, the saddlery and cobblers. Even when freshly created there is something about Bawden's pictures (eclogues really) that seems on the point of fading, as if the artist had known everything is ephemeral. I look at his tariff cards for grand seaside hotels, his beer bottle labels and catalogues for department stores, and there is such melancholy. I suppose it's because he got into his stride during the war – and was an official War Artist – when the way of life he was recording was indeed in grave danger. But the tradition he belongs to is more ancient than that. Bawden's pictures may be grouped with the Canterbury pilgrims dancing their way towards death, the songs of nightingales and skylarks soon to fall silent in Romantic verse, Blake's sick rose, Tennyson's gloom, Elgar's Worcestershire wind-in-the-willows plangency, Britten's folksong arrangements. It is about the spirit of human loss, conveyed by Bawden in his depiction of shabby redbrick houses and ornament-crammed rooms. I feel exactly the same way myself, when I look in the window of Buggle & Sons – at the coils of string and hand-tools and sun-yellowed cards of combs and hair-grips.

Bawden conscientiously recorded country crafts and tools – commonplace goods like nails and screws, bicycles, bedsteads, fenders and junk-filled yards. His father was an ironmonger in Braintree, Essex, which is where he'd have first observed the boxes of horse pills and drums of sheep drench, the packets of seeds and bundles of tallow candles. What I particularly notice about his work – it is never spring or summer. His towns and villages are wet and cold. His biographer Malcolm Yorke said Bawden didn't like the countryside when it became too green, and he never steeped his work in the sentimental, the langorous. Actually, there is a distinct and certain hardness – both literally in the black ink lines and edges of his linocuts and drawings and metaphorically in his subject matter. Often in the background you'll spot spiders trapping flies, cats stalking their prey. It could be said that the theme of feeding extends also to the Fortnum's catalogues and the decorated menus he produced, e.g. for The Pavilion in Scarborough, as owned by Charles Laughton's family. I prefer Bawden any day of the week to Francis Bacon, who couldn't draw properly for arseholes – though paradoxically arseholes was his one big subject.

~

Anna had a busy day even by her extreme standards. Up at 5.30 a.m. to prepare for her church warden duties, counting the hymn books, washing the old ladies' spittle off the chalices, that kind of thing. Did the 8 a.m. Holy Communion Service and the 10 a.m. Morning Worship, complete with Bolivian nose-flutes. She then went to Hereford to run a car boot sale, making a grand total of £63.80. This followed by a session at the gym. In the afternoon, she superintended the Festival of Remembrance Service, plus had to do the associated clearing up, folding the British Legion flags, resuscitating war veterans, filling the tea urn and so forth. She came home to put the laundry on and match up hundreds of pairs of odd socks. Meanwhile the lazy useless children stayed in bed – in my role as lazy useless husband I stayed in bed, too, writing an article of the history of BBC light entertainment and making notes on Julie Walters' autobiography for a review. Coincidentally, when Anna was an infant in Halesowen, Julie was a few streets away as a teenager in Bearwood. Also in the vicinity was Bill Oddie, who grew up in Quinton. This is something fascinating I can bring up at the next neighbours' drinks do, when I've run into the ground with ammonites and Corsica.

~

When the eleven o'clock alarm bell went off to commemorate the Armistice, Anna was in the changing room at T.K. Maxx and had to stand stock still with her knickers on her head.

~

Joyce Crozier of Grandstand Road bought some tomato plants at a charity stall, which have grown into outlandish shapes, or so she told fellow members of Holmer Women's Institute. "I like gardening and I've always grown tomatoes and lovely peppers, but I've never seen anything like this before," said aghast grandmother Mrs Crozier.

~

Sébastien comes in through the door most days with his mobile in his hand, furiously texting. He and his cronies sit on the school bus, texting each other. Nobody takes the trouble to talk to each other properly anymore. Like I am sure every other adolescent of his generation, he completely ignores his parents. We could be the other side of a screen, not quite in focus. To get him to come down from his lair for dinner, I have to phone him up. I go for months without speaking to any of my editors, too – all communication is done in cyberspace, briskly and brutally. I fear we shall soon evolve into blobby lumps (and I'm well on the way) with no extremities save prongs on our foreheads to tap the keyboard. Wit and fluency and conversation are going the way of thatching and sailing ships – quaint and outmoded skills. The best I now hope for from even intelligent fellows is an ill-spelled and ill-phrased three line email. What do I mean *three lines*! I lately spent a few weeks polishing a long article. I proudly sent it off. Silence. Here in its entirety is the grudging response I got eventually: "Ta."

Nobody replies to letters. I am certainly the last person left to use a red pillar box except for at Christmas. I am also the last person to go in for watermarked paper, blue-black Quink ink, sealing wax. A love of stationery played a large part in my wanting to be a writer. Anna and I got together thirty years ago through a joint interest in calligraphy, amongst other things. Christ and a bear you must think I sit here wearing a wig like Doctor Johnson, calling for my goose quills, clay pipe and serving wench – but it's not that I'm antiquated. I'd just prefer a little more courtesy and decorum to come back. Here's an instance of what I mean. When I had luncheon with a distinguished executive from a non-terrestrial digital primetime cable channel recently, she kept poking and prodding at her Handheld BlackBerry, at first semi-surreptitiously under the table and then in full view, brazenly, between mouthfuls. I felt like grabbing the device and throwing it out on the street, under the wheels of a bendy bus. How would she have liked it if I'd plopped a pile of parchment on the banquette and started to inscribe my own office memoranda? Socially, people conduct relationships through Facebook and MySpace. Or else they Twitter and Tweet. I can't abide the brusqueness and the disconnection – and what it all says about the endemic mistrust of real encounters. People are having sex with computers now. It is one step up from those rubber dolls they used to sell in Soho – a few crude slots and reactions. Nothing more.

~

Over the years The Old Penny has changed hands numerous times. I remember when it was run by an ex-submariner covered with tattoos. Then there was a stop-gap with a former regimental-sergeant-major in Queen Alexandra's Royal Army Nursing Corps as the proprietor, who refused to believe me when I said Dijon mustard wasn't the same thing as English mustard. I was virtually put on a charge. Then it became a Thai restaurant, The Old Satang. The daughter died within hours when the GP failed to diagnose total liver failure. She was buried in a wicker coffin and when the light shone through it at the funeral you could see the corpse. Next it was The Old Siam, the people leaving suddenly in a welter of unpaid bills. Now it is Foxy's Steak Bar. The cook said she has to do the steaks in huge cast iron woks. There were free drinks on opening night and Anna asked for sparkling water. We are still quarrelling about this.

~

To see Jane Ashton, an old university chum, for luncheon. She's been in her new house in Evesham for over a year, but could have moved in that morning, the furniture yet to arrive. Not an ornament or picture or sign of occupation. No curtains. Our voices echoed in the kitchen. How very different from my own cluttered home, the wax flowers under glass domes, pinned butterfly collections, suits of armour, Sylvac Face-Pots, Conder lithographs, Venetian masks, toucan-shaped salad tossers, mismatched chipped blue china jugs, Peter Sellers posters, Mrs Mills LPs (Craig is very envious that I found *Mrs Mills' Piano Singalong*, her classic of 1974, so I've left it to him in my Will) and the rest of the ten-thousand-tons of accumulated undusted wild shite. Stopped clocks, which now and again chime thirteen at midnight. A packet of unplanted tomato seeds from Christian Aid. I do my best to live up to my bric-a-brac. But these people who prefer minimalist chambers – what does the non-bric-a-brac say about them? Jane has a dog called Pip with a deformed paw.

~

Later in the week, I covered my salad with marmalade. I'd bought the jar at the St Michael's Day Hospice Christmas Fête and misread *chutney* for *chunky*. Duncan said the same thing happened to him. He spread Vaseline on his toast. I said don't say another single word. I am sticking my fingers in my ears if you do. But it had something innocently to do with his contact lenses and clouded honey.

~

At the St. Michael's Day Hospice Christmas Fête in the ballroom at The Ptarmigan, I was examining some greetings cards. "All done with beeswax," said the lady. "But these are the last." "You've run out of bees?" I asked, wondering how that could happen. "I've got carpal tunnel syndrome," the lady explained, "and a trapped nerve in my back that gives me water retention. I'm on morphine."

December

To a swish and neurotically hip party in Mayfair that was straight out of George Grosz and Otto Dix. Lots of bosomy young girls in strapless gowns and hordes of horrible flabby old blokes, amongst whom Gyles and me. The Brandreth jewels had evidently come up from the vault for the evening as Mrs Gyles was there, looking like Elektra in a Viennese theatre production directed by Hugo von Hoffmannsthal, circa 1900. Mrs Gyles' job was to be charming to Ed Victor, whom I last saw decades ago, when he was trying to be charming to Iris Murdoch – an uphill task as she was in the Land of Far Beyond with the Alzheimer's, though he did secure her as a client. Gyles introduced me to David Cameron, whom I kept calling James, as if he was the director of *Titanic*. That out-gay over-groomed MP Alan Duncan was talking to a girl in a white fur stole. "Oh," I said. "Untouched pussy. You don't see much of that in the West

End." They looked at me daggers. Had I been a recognisable or famous face, they'd have laughed uproariously – as it was, my remark was sheer impertinence. I noticed Andrew Roberts was earnestly chatting to the head of BBC Radio Four. Andrew always confuses me with my cousin Jeremy – an easy mistake to make, as Jeremy is over six-foot-tall with a posh voice and is covered with corduroy and I'm a dark South Welsh dwarf. Roberts spoke to me briefly, before giving me a baboon grimace and turning on his little heel to carry on basking in the company of the beetle-browed and uncompromisingly bald Mark Damazer – the grimace of a baboon with diarrhoea trying to hold it in, if you want me to be precise.

It was a party for people who are assiduous in the social climbing department – for bankers and fat cats and advertisers who will now be hiding away in Switzerland whilst the rest of us pick up the pieces. The guests were like a bundle of slithering snakes and prancing spiders in a granite cave, only distantly related to human life. Piers Morgan was at large of course, symbolising all that is degrading about the modern print media. He misled his *Daily Mirror* readers by publishing hoax photographs of British soldiers abusing Iraqi prisoners, got himself sacked, got himself famous, and got on television, which is what he wanted. I found it a deeply dispiriting night – everyone howling and yelling and not listening to each other, nothing anyone said being designed to be actually heard for a single second. I longed to be a cackling knitter manning a guillotine. Nothing here was going to tend to anything good, yet it was getting the guests' adrenaline going.

～

Tristan and I left at 9.30 and went to St. Alban in Lower Regent Street, where the interior is like the saloon in the *QE2*, when the ship was first launched in 1967. St. Alban opened two years ago and hasn't quite caught on yet, as it always seems pretty empty. Unless the clientele clears out of the backdoor and piles through the toilet windows whenever I saunter in at the front. Perhaps people think it is in the town of St Albans and can't be bothered to make the trek to remote Hertfordshire? The front-of-house chap, Everard Mitchell, or is it Mitchell Everard, is always nice to me, but he wasn't on duty tonight. Tristan was wearing a top hat, and instead of looking like a toff he was mistaken for a hotel doorman and people expected him to hail cabs for them, which he did.

～

As may be well anticipated, German-born caricaturist and social satirist George Grosz was banned by the Nazis as "Cultural Bolshevist Number One" and so ran away to New York. He returned to Berlin in 1959 saying "my American dream turned out to be a soap bubble," and died there shortly after his arrival following a fall down a flight of stairs. I quizzed Gyles, who knows bloody everything, what is it therefore that connects George Grosz and Derek Nimmo? "Were they both born in a caravan outside Liverpool?" he answered.*

~

If George Grosz was "Cultural Bolshevist Number One," I'm Number Two.

~

A real crime wave here. You'll remember that plastic swan episode up Elmsdale Road? Police are now "baffled by a bizarre bedsit burglary" – though evidently not by an outbreak of alliteration. A 50cm Beswick horse has gone missing. "It is brown in colour with a black mane, tail and hooves." Anyone with information should contact PC Adele Loney, who is in charge of the forensic team dusting for prints. My theory is that Professor Moriarty is at the back of all of it, purring over his menagerie of plastic swans and pottery ponies whilst sipping tea brewed using Age Concern's kettle, as that was never found either. He probably fished Vinny Hilton's false leg out of the Wye and is using that for evil purposes too. Buy a consignment of *The Whiz* from the man ("a breakthrough in comfort & convenience for women"), your tuppence will explode. I can't wait for the re-enactment on *Crimewatch*. They could cast Hob and Knob, Hob in a special effects costume as *The Whiz* and Knob balancing on the mantelpiece as a 50cm Beswick horse. Can't you just *see* it?

*Historical note. Derek Nimmo, best known as a bungling monk in the clerical comedy *Oh Brother!* and always in demand on the after-dinner -speaking circuit, died in February 1999, aged sixty-nine, as a result of toppling down some steps.

~

What with my farting and Anna's snoring, our bedroom to a casual passer-by must sound like the rehearsal hall for Herb Alpert and the Tijuana Brass. Anna has now been diagnosed with sleep apnoea, and according to the leaflet distributed by the quack, "The sort of person who most commonly suffers from heavy snoring and sleep apnoea is an overweight middle-aged man with a large neck, usually with a size 17-inch collar or more." Well, I've got the as-described body, Anna's got the ailment. We are always psychosomatically exchanging infirmities in this fashion. When she had the ovaries out, I had a guts ache. I was the first father known to medical science who nearly died in childbirth. They wanted to put me in *The Lancet*. Anyway, Anna had to collect an oxygen mask device from the department of respiratory investigation at the County Hospital. She has to truss herself up with tubes and pipes to a whirring engine and attach wires and clips to her fingers. Pity the poor burglar materialising in our bedroom in the small hours – it would be like stumbling upon the abominable Dr. Phibes' experiment chamber.

The world being very small – who should the sleep apnoea nurse be but only the mother of Amy Tortue, the Montmartre tap dancer, whom Tristan recently dumped, amidst many tears and much bitterness. What an ideal opportunity, therefore, for a loving mother's revenge. I told Anna to check the face mask for concealed scorpions.

~

To Hope Pickles' for Christmas drinks. I must say, there seems to be a curse on me where visiting her family is concerned. I got well twatted on the Rioja and scratched *Cunty Fuck* in the frost on a car window as we made our way back to our Volvo. I can see now that this was carrying the writer's compulsive need to write a shade *too far*. Well, it only turned out to be Hope Pickles' dad's car – and he's a police sergeant in Kidderminster. So Anna had to drive back and I had to try and creep along the pavement like Richard Burton in *Where Eagles Dare* to erase the evidence of my moment of madness. As there are CCTV cameras everywhere these days there are bound to be repercussions. My professorships and doctorates will be rescinded. The governor of Kentucky will strip me of my colonel's commission. The last thing I did like that was in 1978 when I filled a pillar box in Bassaleg, South Wales, with tongue sandwiches.

~

Fair play to the Pickles family, though. Their dog is called Branston. Branston had what I thought was an old-fashioned alarm clock strapped to his collar, but then why would a dog need to tell the time? It is a homing device of some kind, which zaps him with the alternating current if he strays beyond the garden and on to the A44 to Worcester. The odd thing is, the wattage or voltage or frequency setting (or whatever – children with GCSE science will know) is exactly the same as the dishwasher – and when the cycle reaches its climax, poor old Branston foams at the mouth and runs around the ceiling. Is this unusual, do you think, for one's pets to be assaulted by a kitchen appliance, not low-grade tingles either, but Gestapo-strength electric shocks? From Branston's point-of-view it is a cartoon nightmare world, of furniture and brooms and cutlery coming alive.

~

Harold Pinter obit. What a ghastly clanking beast he was, with eyeballs blacker than anthracite. I wonder if future biographers will make anything of the fact that I shared the lift at the National Theatre once with him and Victor Spinneti? (Ned Sherrin might have concocted a splendid after-dinner anecdote.) Pinter's personality was a black storm, too. Paul Bailey for example, reviewed one of his radio plays for *The Listener*, writing his notice in a parody of Pinter's laconic style. Forty years later, Paul sees Pinter emerging from the gents at the Royal Academy. "Don't think I've *fucking* forgotten," said the dramatist. He tried to have a diner thrown out of the River Café, believing him to be a journalist or secret policeman. Actually it was a chap who was planning to propose to his girlfriend that evening. And at Caroline Michel and Matthew Evans' Wedding of the Century, Nobel Prize Winner and typical Libran Harold Pinter started screaming and stormed off – he'd been going on about *fucking* South America and *fucking* South American tin pot dictators, and who should be sitting next to him but the wife of Mario Vargas Llosa.

"You seem to know a lot about my country," she said at last. "Yes, more than you do, you *cunt*!" he replied, and refused to apologise. Lady Antonia carried on doing her Queen Mother trick of beaming obliviously and seraphically into the middle-distance, a creature of the starry welkin.

I always found it very suspect, the way Pinter would write about oppression in faraway lands and under distant regimes, and yet he'd take it out on waiters and taxi drivers in London. He couldn't be happy unless at some point during the day he'd snarled *fuck* or *cunt* at someone he'd decided was beneath him. On his very last outing to a restaurant, before the cancer got him, he rallied enough to be able to yell "What a stupid *fucking* question!" when asked if he'd prefer sparkling water or still water. He was oblivious to bruised feelings – indifferent to the individuals around him. His first wife and muse Vivian Merchant drank herself to death when he abandoned her for Lady Antonia. He never had much humanity that I could see, yet the papers are unanimous that here is the passing of our greatest playwright.

How can that opinion possibly be sustained? Beckett got there first, with the claustrophobic intensity. I suppose the early plays are suitable for revival and entertain sixth forms; works such as *The Birthday Party* and *The Caretaker* and *The Homecoming*, with their details about cornflakes and sour milk, the dank kitchenettes and bed-sitting rooms. But it is all gloom and weight, with no lightness. Which is why for me our best dramatist is Alan Bennett, who'll never win The Nobel because he possesses a comic spirit.

Nevertheless, there are marked similarities between the writers, as it happens. Bennett's lower-middle class Leeds upbringing was similar to Pinter's in Hackney, and both were drawn ever-after to the search for evidence of refinement – the installation of an indoor lavatory, the use of doilies, attendance at coffee mornings and poetry readings, the ability to afford felt-underlay, arrange flowers and to pronounce *steak diane*.

Pinter and Bennett were both professional actors, giving them an awareness of their tricks and effects, especially the tone of the voice. Pinter once played Sir Lancelot Spratt, and I think that does explain him – the wrathful and preposterous surgeon, as famously incarnated by the bombastic James Robertson Justice. Bennett's deliberate persona is that of the bachelor clergyman or old-style don, who can rhapsodise about mixed biscuits, cork flooring, gasometers and wraparound pinnies with the scholarliness of a professor of medieval history – something he might have become, had not *Beyond the Fringe* diverted him. As a junior lecturer at Magdalen, he taught Bevis Hillier, future magisterial biographer of Sir John Betjeman.

I infinitely prefer Bennett's Leeds and Morecambe to Pinter's anonymous torture chambers, yet here again the authors shared the same dilemmas, as they contemplated matters of life and death, forgetfulness and dementia. "Don't go calling Dr. Swaby. He'll put me away ... Dr. Swaby put Mrs Beevers away. He asked her for the name of the prime minister, she didn't know and he carted her off to Low

Moor," bleats the mother in abject fear in *A Private Function*, a role played by the blissful Liz Smith. "Dr. Swaby told her she was going to Bridlington. She ended up in Low Moor. It was her house." The menacing night visitors in Pinter, the notorious thugs and charmers who turn up unannounced and uninvited – in Bennett's plays, also, people fear the equivalent men in white coats, the strangers from the Council or the Corporation, who'll come and take you away, incarcerate you in a retirement home or an intensive care ward.

Social workers order old people about, unseen managers order employees about. "I ran into Mr Butterfield in planning and he says a question mark definitely hangs over Ipswich," is a line in Bennett's *Green Forms*, but it could be from the realm of Kafka – and Bennett has written two whole plays about Kafka, *The Insurance Man* and *Kafka's Dick*. In Bennett's *Enjoy* and Pinter's *No Man's Land* – both running in the West End as I write – everyone is being monitored and shadowed. The works have in common a theme of people being pushed about against their will; they have to cope with change and uncertainty; they are assessed and logged and records are going to be kept by intruders and government inspectors. Knowing this, the characters hope to be taken for a better class of person, boasting about champagne and scrambled eggs and finger buffets, and they maintain that they can still, despite the lies and rumours, use the toilet unassisted. Everybody is desperately keeping up appearances, as if their very lives depend upon it.

~

Parenthetically, who do Sir Michael Gambon's agents and representatives think he is being these days, taking over roles originated by either Sir Ralph Richardson or Sir Laurence Olivier? I hope they don't think he's their equivalent or equal? Richardson played Hirst at the National in 1975, and Gambon's Lord Marchmain in a recent adaptation of *Brideshead Revisited* wasn't a patch on Olivier in the John Mortimer version of 1982. He has played Archie Rice, too though I didn't see it*. There is a fatal playfulness to a Gambon performance — as though *he* knows that *we* know that *he* knows this acting business is only a silly game of Let's Pretend. He is disengaged from the essential nature of his own chosen art form — which is what makes him interesting and mesmerising. Part of him is elsewhere, unreachable. He tantalises us — particularly in interviews, where he gives nothing away. (Apparently he is a qualified engineer. How many other mimes could fix your washing machine?) Gambon has an enviably frivolous soul — as how else to explain the way he put on a bright red wig to portray Oscar Wilde?

~

Barry Cryer phones and says that he was in a garden centre and overheard a man say, "That sundial I bought last year has nearly paid for itself." We spent ages trying to work out

---

*In a production of *The Entertainer* on BBC2 in 1994 Bill Owen was Billy Rice, Billie Whitelaw was Phoebe. The only person called Billy or Billie not involved was Billy Smart.

quite what this might mean or entail. Barry also had two great jokes. A woman goes into a pet shop to buy a parrot. The man says, "This parrot is cheap because it used to live in a brothel and I can't guarantee what it might come out with." The woman says she'll risk it. Takes the parrot home. The parrot looks around and says, "Nice room. Very comfortable and romantic. Cosy." The woman's daughters come in. "Oh, some nice new girls. Lovely." Her husband comes in. "Hello Keith !" You think it is going to be about the parrot swearing and it's not. You're wrong-footed. Also, *Keith* is funny, for some reason.

Second tale. A man goes into a sex shop and browses around the shelves. He says to the assistant, "Have you got one of these big penises that's really a candle?" "Well we do as a matter of fact." "Best light it then. I've come to cut the electricity off." Again, you'd not have seen that dénouement coming. Barry and I debate and pore over the art and science of comedy with the passion of F.R. Leavis or egghead genius Christopher Ricks leading and illuminating seminars on Bob Dylan's sonnets. The best remark we ever had to ponder was this: "I can forgive, but I can't knit."

～

A surreal moment in the Co-op. A West Highland Terrier fell out of a woman's coat and into the chest freezer, where it ran around the McCain's Oven Chips. It was a cold day, so she'd tried to smuggle the pooch into the shop, doing it a kindness. The staff went mental and I had a good laugh.

～

Oscar's friends have names like debt collectors and remittance men in Dickens – Trigg, Jibb, Beech, Monsoon and Measle. Measle is in a band where Kuba, the bass guitarist and lead singer, is Polish and puts the emphasis randomly on the wrong words in the non-hit number, "Buy A Tee-Shirt With My Face." Oscar went to hear the band, which calls itself *Holy Circus*, play in Hay-on-Wye on New Year's Eve. Also in evidence were their arch-rivals, *Foetus Christ*. One of their lyrics is "Shakin' grass/playin' fast". Oscar came back covered with an orange rash – he'd spent the night on the floor of a house that was full of gerbils, mice, budgies and lizards and he was bitten by the mites and fleas.

~

Oscar's new squeeze Tess has luscious baps. Except she hasn't. "They're implants." "Eggplants?" "No, *implants*, Dad." Apparently if you tap them with a spoon they clink or chink, like knocking on Warden Hodges' ARP tin helmet. The sad thing is, the poor girl is still only in her teens – but the joke is that the £4,000 operation was paid for by her ex-boyfriend, whom she dumped before he could have a proper good go with them. He should ask for a refund. It would be difficult to ask for them back.

~

As for my own New Year's Day – as Kenneth Williams said, before taking the overdose, *what's the bloody point?* First, there was no hot water. Secondly, I received a letter from Capital One imposing a default charge of £12 because the £1.04 due reached my account on 27 December rather than

24 December. Then Sébastien blocked the toilet and I had to poke it with a stick. Next a royalty statement arrived from Faber showing that a full six years after the publication of my much-misunderstood Anthony Burgess biography, £58,346.83 of the original £60,000 advance remains to be cleared. Seven copies were sold last year worldwide. I am in the curious position of being able to know my entire readership by name. The reason why I was long since dropped from the Faber Summer Party list is finally revealed. Stephen Page and Lee Brackstone must cross themselves and sprinkle Holy Water about whilst mumbling prayers if my name gets mentioned. Later, I spent three full hours ordering a Dell ink cartridge from a person in Bombay who kept calling me *miss*. After the first hour it got too embarrassing to insist on a correction. But do I *honestly* sound like I've got a *vagina*?

~

It goes on. Light bulbs pop as I pass by them – I don't mean go out and need replacing. I mean they explode and launch themselves from the socket at my face like bombs, fizzing and leaving a little trail of hot coals. This has happened with three different lamps in as many days. If the toaster gets it into its head to commence hostilities, I'm a goner. Finally, as I finished transferring this manuscript to my laptop, the computer hard drive went kaput. The screen pinged and went blank. I knew what Thomas Carlyle went through, when the maid used the original manuscript of *The French Revolution* as spills to ignite the kitchen fire. I felt a kinship with my hero the legendary Anthony Burgess, too, who had a briefcase containing the only typescript of *Joysprick: An Introduction to the Language of James Joyce* stolen in Rome by *scippatori*, those pairs of muggers who buzz past on Vespas and Lambrettas, snatching at mink stoles and handbags. We can safely assume that when Burgess's *scippatori* got home that night and discovered what they'd nicked they would have been wearing very long faces.

Mine was a problem no normal nerd or geek could cope with – I had to go to the police station and ask who the forensic data recovery people are whom they use when examining the computers of paedophiles and Islamic bombers. I reasoned that if they can find out what Gary Glitter and the Taliban are up to, when such villains know what they're doing when they delete stuff intentionally, they can fucking well recover *Seasonal Suicide Notes*. At a cost to me of £1,437.50, that I don't have, expert engineers spent twenty hours performing brain surgery on my apparatus and duly plucked the very book you are holding in your mittens from the depths of the computer's cerebral cortex, or possibly the stratosphere. It was altogether the worst thing to have happened to me since my father died – quite dizzymaking. Computers are voodoo really, and I had everything to fear, the least of it being that my visit to the police station might be misconstrued and I have now inadvertently placed myself on the Sex Offenders' Register and in the queue for Guantanamo Bay. Will I look good in the orange jerkin? How well will I cope with torture and being a black man's bitch? I can't go to jail M'Lud because my haemorrhoids won't stand it. Nonetheless in spite of everything I dream I'm on a plinth in Trafalgar Square, and Anna keeps complaining that I wake her up at night because in my sleep I keep laughing hysterically. Well, it is only when asleep that I can view my life from afar.

~

If you want to see the world in its true light, watch old episodes of *Crossroads*. The dullness is the dullness of real life – observe how the camera records a character silently and slowly pouring tea into six or maybe sixteen cups, then the milk, then the sugar; be mesmerised by Meg Richardson dialling a twenty-digit long-distance number on the big white phone, only to have to hang up; marvel at the look of growing incredulity on Sandy's face as he taps at a pocket calculator for minutes on end and then announces, "Have you *seen* how the price of tinned *coffee* has gone up *three times* this quarter *alone*!" We are watching time being deliberately killed. Compared with the hopelessness and inconsequentiality of life as it is lived in *Crossroads*, other dramas from Aeschylus to Sir David Hare seem just too crafted and honed. Though recognised as works of art they are, by comparison, well, artificial. Pinter and his famous pauses were I always felt as nothing when put side-by-side with the reception desk hoop-la at a Midlands motel, and *Crossroads* to this day can be said to symbolise the blithe indifference of an unbalanced, random cosmos, where nothing is finally knowable.

Crossroads left the boredom and the errors and the hesitancies in, and I find this soothing. Ann George's lines were written out on beer mats, which she lifted up and peered at whilst pretending to dust. The dialogue was muffed and door handles fell off and it was necessary on occasion for people to come and go through the fireplace. "Every exit," said Sir Tom Stoppard, "is an entrance somewhere else." But not on *Crossroads* they weren't. Benny went to fetch a spanner and vanished for six months without explanation. In 1987 he climbed up a ladder to attend to the Christmas fairy and never came down. Epicene chef Bernard Booth said, "If anyone wants me, I'll be in the storeroom," and only re-appeared after a full year, not even looking rumpled. Sally Adcock, who played a Salvation Army motel waitress, also went into a store cupboard in 1979 – and permanently de-materialised. Frumpy Glenda Barlow tottered off to the lavatory and sat there for seven months. Arthur Brownlow headed off to his bowls club – he never came home.

Because of the pervasive near-imbecility, mostly these disappearing acts were (spookily) never discussed or even alluded to, but we would for some reason be told that Wee Shughie McFee was in the kitchen or busy on the phone, when in fact Angus Lennie, the actor, was absolutely nowhere to be seen. "I was able to go off and do other things," he said. Amy Turtle was accused of being a Russian spy called Amelia Turtlovski and went to Texas for twelve years, allowing Ann George to do pantomime. When Roger

Tonge died in 1981, Sandy was said rather tastelessly to have "gone on holiday."

Thousands of people used to write in to the television company, asking where they could buy Meg Richardson's wallpaper and curtain fabrics, or whether they could hire the motel and have their wedding reception there, with Bernard Booth and Wee Shughie McFee doing the catering. (The illusion is kept going in a volume published in 1977 "by arrangement with ATV Limited" called *The Crossroads Cookbook* – "After his trip to Turkey with Kelly, David Hunter should be an expert on kebabs.") People would apply for jobs as waitresses or washers-up and send in baby clothes when a cast member was expecting.

Callous bastards may laugh – but I understand absolutely the need to willingly suspend the old disbelief and live so far as it is possible in a parallel universe. I'd loved to have been a guest at the motel myself, dining daily on grapefruit with prawns, crown roast of lamb and chocolate mousse. Perhaps I found an authentic equivalent the other day. I went with Anna to the Holiday Inn, Birmingham, where coincidentally Ann George used to take up residence during her filming stints at the (since demolished) ATV studios. I adored the unreconstructed seventies ambience, complete with carvery. Walnut-brown paint everywhere and plastic ceilings. Trailing pot plants. Singapore airline pilots or stewards still in their uniforms pulling little suitcases on wheels. A rack with leaflets about the Alexandra Theatre.

~

Why can't I dream on demand of, say, circuses? For there is something dreamlike about them always – and something unsettling too. But then dreams *are* disturbing and the circus is a world that comes and goes, it settles for a moment and vanishes, the colourful tents and caravans, the horses floating by as if in slight slow motion, the trumpet notes of the clown dying away as darkness falls on the ring, everybody involved seemingly a creature from another realm or dimension.

Yesterday morning in the Big Top they did a show for London's Orthodox Jewish Community. Two thousand of those bearded characters with the black hats and ringlets. And that's the women. Like a Woody Allen Convention. Or Mel Brooks. I dared the clown, who is Jewish himself, to run into the ring waving a bacon sandwich. There was a van selling "Uncle Doovy's Kosher Ice Cream." Instead of the usual ice cream van jingles, the noises emerging from it were the wails and balalaika stuff you get in synagogues. No female performers were allowed. Nothing even slightly risqué. The lady trapeze artistes and the clown's wife, who is Hungarian (and who grew up in Budapest in the bad old days), all had to hide in their caravans and seethe, banished for (the word that's used) their immodesty. I said, "I've got the only foreskin in miles." When I lustily started to sing a chorus of "Springtime for Hitler and Germany, Winter for Poland and France…", the clown's wife, who does the face painting, told me she's had these Muslim women coming up to her in full parachute gear and she has to paint little clown

198

or tiger faces in the wee windows of the burquas.

~

At the end of Tristan's season was the graduation showcase. Zippo himself, Martin Burton, was present in a black velvet frock coat, every ample inch the grand impresario. The Ringmaster was the great Norman Barrett, now in his seventies and immaculate in a silk topper. Greg was in a regimental mess-coat with silver buttons and Cossack boots, like an Austro-Hungarian major-general about to invade Bosnia-Herzegovina. He didn't stop patrolling the edge of the ring, checking and double-checking the wires and clips.

There were a lot of nerves backstage I gather. But what a night it was. Ian Jarvis had developed into a true charismatic performer, swinging and leaping off straps and ropes, suspending Jackie Armstrong from his ankles or toes. Douglas Fairbanks or Errol Flynn were not more swashbuckling. Ian had become, so I understand, quite the circus Casanova, with a flock of female fans in each venue. Male fans too I should imagine. Tommaso hopped about with a Chinese parasol. A Norwegian called Carola Wisney had a nice mime act involving balloons. Carola happens to be deaf – and quite a contingent had turned up to support her from Oslo. They wiggled their hands and did a lot of sign language – Norwegian sign language at that – whether egging Carola on or excitedly sharing the latest gossip with her about salmon fishing quotas and fjords we'll never know.

The tension created by a live flesh-and-blood show can't be replicated in any television recording. We'd be filled with fear – and then there's this gush of relief that such dare devilry hasn't led to crumpled bodies in the sand. Then Mr Twix came on. Tristan opened a Fortnum's hamper and juggled with the picnic utensils. He then did some fancy juggling with his hat – he'd seen W.C. Fields do this with a straw boater. He put a cylinder on a box, a plank on the cylinder, and balanced himself on it whilst rolling about and juggling with five red balls. He then produced a shiny white ball – from *where?* – and juggled with that, too. We clapped until our hands were sore, even though he dropped stuff and wasn't at his best.

Afterwards there were the prizes. Ian won a big silver cup for his achievements. Tristan won the Charlie Cairoli Award, presented by the Charlie Cairoli Appreciation Society to the Best Comedy Performer. Martin has now offered him a proper job, if he wants it. We went to the bar and when the generators were switched off at midnight we stood chatting in the darkness of the ring, the students' faces lit up by the sheer thrill of having lived up to the level of their ideals. Beyond the realistic surface of their physical achievements, for a few hours they'd known what it is like to have a mythical presence, a supernatural aura. There was quite a becoming Fellini feel to the mood, too – the Big Top at night lit by the moon, the smudged make up, an underlying forlornness that something had ended, the close-knit group inevitably dispersing. Conversation was of the circus legends people had seen or heard about – the Wallendas, who a hundred feet up would balance on each other's shoulders and turn somersaults; Blondin, who cooked an omelette whilst traversing a tight-rope; Sir Robert Fossett, who'd put on a blindfold and jump on and off a galloping horse; Zacchini, the Mighty Human Canonball, who lost consciousness as he flew through the air and regained consciousness a moment before landing in the safety net; the brave dwarves who'd leapt through hoops of fire... It was after two in the morning when I eventually walked away, and when I looked back from under a streetlamp to wave at Tristan, he had already gone.

2009

YOU'LL REMEMBER THE ROKEBY VENUS ? I was the one holding the mirror. Suffice it to say, looks have been lost since. I know this because I've been pestered throughout the year for one reason and another by photographers – none of whom despite their best efforts with filters and wide-angle lenses smeared with Nivea can make me look half-human or any prettier than a butch lesbian icon. For the *Guardian* I was lit from below and Barry Cryer thought it was Aleister Crowley, the Satanist. The *Daily Mail* made me into a drugged Chinese illusionist. The *Sunday Times* caught me in my study – it was as if Stratford Johns had been disturbed during a mid-morning crap. They came back again and I had to don a Santa suit. Did Sir Vidia have to don a Santa suit to win the Nobel Prize for Literature? Answer me that. Fucking *did he*? In *OK Magazine*, papped at Michael Winner's party, readers must have assumed I was a care-in-the-community pre-op causing a drunken disturbance.

I take some solace in the fact I am heading for a Double-Z-List Celebrity Ranking, some way below the person who came fourth in *Big Brother* (Series Five) and who went to hell and back, but slightly above Simon Groom, the awkward *Blue Peter* presenter. And my word, with tits like mine and the right agent I could be a star. Yet these professional photographers, one of them a flamboyant, genuine Italian, named if I am not mistaken Giovanni Battista Tiepolo*, would have been better off doing blow-ups of the funny-shaped carrots people used to send in to Esther. I've had to pose against walls, up alleys, in fields, in graveyards, adjacent to shops – and adjacent to a sign saying Winter Pansies Now On Sale. *Pansies* spelt *pansy's* of course. All in aid of peddling the First Edition Hardback of *Seasonal Suicide Notes*, already available on Amazon for £1.63, slashed from £12.99. Does anyone understand the wisdom of such economics? At £1.63 I'm hardly a collector's item, am I? Even Michael Winner's *Winner's Dinners* is priced at £8.61, though many of his copies are autographed.

More often than not the picture editors back at base take one look at the sorry bunch of snaps and decide to scrub the whole shoot and run a portrait of Sad Mother Julie Myerson, 48, instead. This will be because of our by-now fabled exchange, discussed back at the start of this book. "Is writing what you do full time? Sorry I ought to know this," she once said to me – to which I replied, very temperately I thought, "Arseholes to you, then." This has become my Lake Isle of Innisfree. My "They fuck you up your mum and dad." My

---

*In fact, the award-winning Francesco Guidicini. Dr Lewis must have his little joke.

cast-iron candidate for an entry in the next edition of *The Oxford Dictionary of Quotations*.

January

On the whole, though, becoming a butch lesbian icon and a care-in-the-community pre-op causing a drunken disturbance at Michael Winner's parties notwithstanding, it has been an uneventful year. I am the Emily Dickinson of Pump Street. Week upon week I go nowhere. I do nothing. Wobbling along to the Co-op in the mild drizzle to buy oven chips is enough to herald a Red Letter Day. Once, I pushed the boat out and bought a mandarin orange flan too. I really did. Compared to me, Emily Dickinson was a Jazz Age flapper, a dirty stop-out. "How dreary to be somebody!/How public, like a frog/To tell your name the livelong day/To an admiring bog." Cheers, Emily.

~

I have failed glaringly in one area. I have not managed to stamp out the round-robin. Still these smug, boastful, transcendentally tedious yet inadvertently side-splitting photocopied Christmas Letters keep arriving. The Queen Mother's former flower arranger at Birkhall tells us that "this is the first year in nearly 40 years that I haven't sailed in a P & O or Cunard ship," and a cathedral organist of my acquaintance cheered everyone up by announcing that he'd had a stroke, his wife is in a wheelchair with diabetes, and his daughter's breast cancer has spread – spread all over Abergavenny. "Have a lovely Christmas," he yet managed to entreat. An old fart in Chester told us they had "a bumper crop of apples and tomatoes and a beautiful show of autumn dahlias... A new heating system was installed when the thermostat on the old Rayburn boiler (25 years old !) gave up the ghost." But who can hope to compete with the ghastly Chinnor family – the saga of Emma's new Prada handbag; the hilarious tale of Emma's birthday treat to see Barry Manilow; Emma's new music room and her adventures with the comical low-class builders; Mark's pre-lunch drinks for local magistrates and his brush with swine flu; the horrible-sounding son Rupert's stubborn preference for Addenbrooke's rather than Massachusetts General Hospital, "one of the five top hospitals in the world. He worked in ER and really saw life." And my eldest son is a *circus clown*.

~

I have cracked the mystery of Gyles Brandreth. He is a set of identical quintuplets. This is how he can run around all at once, giving speeches, mounting Teddy Bear exhibitions, writing thrillers, setting quizzes, having luncheon with Donald Sinden. There is no other possible explanation. Gyles' mother died recently aged 96. If death-defying Mrs Troll follows suit that would mean another twenty years of Mrs Troll, a prospect up with which I cannot put. Perhaps before then compulsory euthanasia will have come in and she can wake up on her birthday to a cake and a surprise injection.

~

The former vicar of Garway with Orcop has converted to the Greek Orthodox Church and has published a book about vampires. "It tells the story of how vampires came into existence and is set during the Roman destruction of Jerusalem." Like reincarnation, vampires and werewolves are now an absolute established scientific fact.

~

I thought I had an advanced melanoma on my foot – I'd trodden on a currant.

~

Oscar and Sébastien to Wolverhampton to see a warbling tramp called Seasick Steve. Do his chums call him Sea or Sick for short? I waited in the car. Anna phoned her sister about 20,000 times, trying to hook up with her for dinner. The excuses we had. Not back from work yet. Back from work but in the shower. Feeding her child. Clearing up from feeding her child. On her way. Nearly on her way. Finally – mission aborted. She said she didn't want to walk in the dark from the car park to the restaurant. My feeling was that she could have said this at the outset – that really and truly she honestly couldn't be arsed. Why do women have to go through this boring dance? Are they all mad or just most of them? Anna's sister lives in Wolverhampton, by choice too.

February

One of the reasons I like Austria is that the police stations are so clean. I tucked myself away in Bad Ischl to write a long piece for the forthcoming master work, *Growing Up With Comedians*, comparing and contrasting Kenneth

Williams and Francis Bacon, a chapter I have called "Scream-ing Popes and Screaming Queens." What this meant in prac-tice was that I did no paid work, as such. There'll be trouble ahead with NatWest, Barclaycard, American Express, etc. If, as somebody said, happiness is being able to meet one's bills, no wonder my face is always longer than Hitler's when he found out the cost of gas.

~

There's a Chinese restaurant in Bad Ischl I just won't be persuaded to enter. Austrian-Chinese cuisine? An hour later you're hungry again for power. (An old joke, sure – but I like it. Mort Sahl's originally? Roald Dahl's? Salvador Dali's? *Hello Dolly*'s?)

~

Crime Wave Corner: A woman in Hereford called Michaela Cheesman has been "left heartbroken" after an ornamental robin was stolen from her mother's grave. "It was one of her favourite birds," said distraught Michaela. "I was horrified, disgusted and saddened to find on my visit to the grave that someone had taken the robin." Horrified, disgusted, sad-dened... She's been at the thesaurus again, old Michaela.

But there are evil forces about. The ornamental robin has clearly gone the way of the Elmsdale Road plastic swan and Age Concern's legendary kettle. The Victims' Support team is run off its feet.

March
With Oscar to Francis Wheen's party at the top of Foyles

to celebrate Francis's partner Julia's definitive biography of Margery Allingham. I very confidently marched us out on to the Charing Cross Road and headed in absolutely the wrong direction. Indeed, my crap sense of direction would have impressed Inspector Clouseau.

~

Anna took the children plus Miss Disa the trapeze artiste to Doolin, on the West coast of Ireland. As I cannot abide those maundering fiddles and folk songs I stayed behind and watched my DVD box set of *The Two Fat Ladies* yet again – and bugger me if they don't end up on the West coast of Ireland listening to maundering fiddles and folk songs, whilst cooking lobsters for nuns.

April

Tristan's first professional season with Zippo's Circus begins in earnest, with a Press Show in Blackheath. I can't get enough of Norman Barrett's budgie act. Budgies driving cars, sliding down slopes, firing cannons. The man deserves to be in the Honours List.* On YouTube you can find Norman doing his budgie act *in French*.

~

Paul B. says he makes jam when he's depressed. He must be suicidal then because he's gone into factory-strength production. There's not a plum to be had in Turnham Green. Our jar was spiked with – he said – lemon juice. I think

*Lo, Norman received the MBE in the 2010 New Year's Honours List.

methadone. I was running around the ceiling after putting Paul's jam on my muffin. The label is designed by Maggi Hamling, which means Paul looks like George Melly. Everything Maggi does ends up looking like George Melly, even her drawings of the sea off Aldeburgh.

~

The novelty candle shop in Bromyard, My Candle Burneth, was under new management as My Candle Shineth, but it hath now finally shutteth. "People in Bromyard only buy candles if there's a blackout," I was told.

~

I receive a letter from my former baby-sitter Mags Curnow, who after an interval of only forty-five years felt she could now complain about the way, when left in her charge, I sat her and her sister Gwyneth down, and her brother Johnny, and made them listen to my solo rendering of the entire vocal score of *Iolanthe*. That is of course the one with the fairies in it – so you can guess what they were thinking and perhaps still are thinking. This was Wales after all. But you'd have thought that such an excruciatingly precocious little bastard would surely have *amounted to something* in his later life. That's the tragedy. I never even got as far as a preliminary audition with D'Oyly Carte.

~

I do get the oddest letters from readers. "Coloplast Direct Wetwipes – excellent for wanking," must be the most unexpected of postcards – after I'd written something about my late father's colostomy bag experiences. Coloplast ought to use that as an advertising slogan, if they've got any gumption. Their wetwipes would sell like hot cakes.

Or – another communication from a reader: "No more than eighteen inches from my right elbow is Elizabeth Mavor's *The Ladies of Llangollen*. Do you know this book? It's about lesbians who enjoyed gardening, so there's hope for both of us." Eh? *Eh?* Anyway I *hate* gardening. No, it is more sweeping than that. I hate *outside*.

~

A new landlord at The Hop Pole, Bromyard. Mr Allan Harland, who used to work for the Queen Mother, though in what capacity I never ascertained, promises "to return it to a good, friendly environment where families and good people can come." During the next three consecutive weekends there were fights, affrays, brawls, smashed windows, and the pavements were awash with blood. A good man got an arm severed and was airlifted to the County Hospital. "My guests are woken up and kept awake by the shouting," complained my chum Sylvia, who runs the rival Falcon Hotel. "They want a reduction in their rates." The police responded by issuing fridge magnets, "in a bid to improve contact with the public".

May

I took veteran novelist Paul B. and the speech-writer to three American Presidents, Stephen Masty, to see Norman's budgie act. At the end of the month I took our old friends the Range Rover Discovery-owning Turners to see

Norman's budgie act, this time in High Wycombe. You can take or leave High Wycombe, which seemed to have been knocked flat for motor vehicles.

~

Anna said that a sign in her office "Please Do Not Leave Anything On The Radiator" had fallen on the radiator.

June
A total blank.

July
To Manchester, not to see Norman's budgie act this time, but to see the Young @ Heart Chorus, those American old-sters who sing and dance and whom I adore. We met a few of them in the bar afterwards – genial little creatures. What do we have in our turn? Morris Men, in the name of Sweet Baby Jumping Jesus and all the Sainted Orphans. When it is Folk Festival here in Bromyard, I can't sleep for the total twats in bells and beards hopping about in clogs and clacking their sticks and rending the night air with their hearty cries of "Whey hey !" I told Sylvia if I was staying as a guest at her place I'd want a reduction in my rates.

~

When you consider how I've turned out you must think I had bad parents. Actually the miracle is that *they* didn't run away from home, what with the Fairy Queen from *Iolanthe* tun-ing up in the dawn South Welsh bog-mist and an LP record of John Reed reciting the Lord Chancellor's "Nightmare" patter song playing non-stop. Anyway, one of my latest niggles is that Barbara Mary Lewis (née George) didn't once go to see her eldest grandchild Tristan performing in his circus, not even when Anna offered to give her a lift there and back. Yet on the other hand she's been all the way to the Shetlands and to Snowdonia on mini-breaks. Without my father to get her to do things she doesn't want to do, Barbara Mary Lewis (née George) doesn't do them. Fair play to her, I suppose. You can't say you don't know where you are with such a person, though I am sure it doesn't reflect particularly well on me that every time the phone rings it arouses the forlorn hope that the police are trying to reach me with the news she's been shot as a double agent in a distant war or knocked off a high mountain peak by an angry goat.

~

One can only but sympathise with Cynthia Perkins, 44, who turned up on her parents' doorstep brandishing a fourteen-inch knife. She took a taxi to her parents' home in Hereford, "told the driver she was going to kill the couple and asked him to come back in ten minutes". Iain Goldacre-Clunes, defending, said that his client was "motivated by revenge" – a plea accepted by the judge at Worcester Crown Court as sounding extremely reasonable. He simply told Cynthia, "to move away from Hereford and stop drinking".

~

The Things You See When You Haven't Got A Gun (1): Frank Skinner in Floral Street.

~

A gypsy woman came to the door selling the usual gypsy merchandise. "That's nice," I said when she opened her bag. "How much is it ?" – "You can't have that. It's my crystal ball." You didn't see that coming, I wanted to reply – but instead I paid £7.50 for a crocheted beige placemat. There's always room for another one of those.

~

Young Antony at The Rosie was more forthright. He told the gypsy woman, and in quite a loud voice too, to fuck right off. A mistake. When he went to Paris to spend an off-peak weekend at the Crillon with a trainee paediatric nurse, Young Antony's ornamental thatched wishing-well burned to the ground. Jumping Jesus and Beagles Bollocks! You curse a gypsy woman back at your peril.

~

Sébastien's Prom Night in Worcester. When did this American High School nonsense come in? The boys self-conscious in shapeless shiny new suits, and the girls over made-up and covered with hair lacquer, tripping over their high heels. The hilarious thing is to arrive by original modes of transport – on a fire engine, astride a lawn mower, by stretch limo, in a horse and carriage. Sébastien brushed aside my idea of a pogo-stick and made his way in on foot, waving a cane that had a glass tube full of vodka hidden in the handle. Hope Pickles intended capping it all by descending from an air balloon – a Barbie doll from a George Frederick Handel opera – but I think her dad Sergeant Pickles dropped her off in his police car, the one that had had "Cunty

213

Fuck" inscribed on it by a madman.

~

Here's a mystery that would test the mettle of Sherlock Holmes. I have thirty-three odd socks. This is more perplexing than "The Riddle of the Dancing Men."

~

Slimming World had a Recruitment Evening, cunningly getting us to go along with the temptation of a Hog Roast. It's Alcoholics Anonymous for guzzlers – a woman confessed to her Curly Wurly addiction and I nearly died laughing. I joined and lost half-a-pound in five weeks, which I put back on. My feet are killing me, incidentally. They won't keep me out of Lin's Wok, the Chinese take-away.

~

Crime Wave Corner: the following items have gone missing – a "distinctive leather jacket", left on the back of a chair in a pub. "Despite a thorough search, the jacket was not found." It has orange silk lining and cross-stitching on the shoulders – there's tasteful for you. If I'd seen it, I'd have set fire to it. Also, tablets "that could slow down heart rate" were among the prescription drugs "stolen from a mobility scooter in Hereford town centre." I sincerely hope there's now a bewildered junkie overdosing on haemorrhoid preparations and incontinence pills.

~

It has been so hot here in the Herefordshire Balkans, my poinsettia thinks it is back in Mexico.

August

We threw a dinner party, a mortifying evening. The woman guest was off her tits before she arrived and the chap, when he left, shoved a twenty pound note into my palm. He tipped the host in a private house! I was speechless – and couldn't bring myself to tell Anna for several days. Then she was speechless. We were both speechless. Helen Keller was a noisy bitch compared with how speechless we'd both become. I said eventually that I'd give the money to charity. But I didn't. I shot up The Rosie and spent it on drinks.

~

Anna is such a regular at these Speed Awareness Courses, she's getting to know the videos of toddlers being mown down by villains doing 35 mph in a 30 mph zone by heart.

~

My sexual life has come completely to an end, which is probably for the best. I was in mid-bonk – and doing a fair impersonation of a purple man dilating his eyes and having a cardiac arrest, a stroke, and going into spastic spasms from rabies simultaneously – when Anna's sweet voice piped up to say, "Did you know there's a VW camper van rally on in Malvern ?" I didn't actually.

~

At Llangrove Garden and Flower Show, Kate Bibby "came out top" in the decorated paper plate category and Mrs Aubrey was photographed "with the beetroot entered by herself and her husband, Philip."

September

Oscar has a job behind the bar in The Rosie, so I'm often there slurping a family-size Lagavulin, talking drivel – as is obligatory in pubs. The locals accord me much respect. They ignore me.

~

The public is being advised "not to touch any of the dead fish" they might find in the River Dore, according to Environment Agency officers. I know a lot of local chefs who will be excited by this news and who shall now be scouring the banks of the River Dore for tonight's Specials.

~

By the time I get around to watching anything on the box it is three in the morning and there is a woman in the corner of the screen gesticulating like billy-o for the benefit of blind people. No that can't be right. Deaf people. You should have seen her expressions when Sir Attenborough's *Life* was on – penguins eating seals, seals eating penguins. Not much in the way of dialogue or informed commentary, but lots of screaming and squawking that needed miming. The poor woman in the corner of the screen was pulling faces and hopping about like an enraged, pop-eyed goblin, i.e. like my mother when inconvenienced in a minor way or beloved housekeeper Mrs Troll on discovering Pinget's rubber bone in the stew cauldron (again). I much preferred watching the signing-for-the-deaf than watching the documentary itself. By the way, what is the matter with Sir Attenborough's voice? It is as if he can't wholly open his mouth, having burnt his tongue on a microwaved sausage.

October

I organised a party for myself and a few friends in the Zippo's Big Top on Hampstead Heath. Booze from Majestic. Food by Anna's mum. Invitations despatched by the blue stockings at Short Books and designed in the style of a circus poster by Emily Grooet Van Tooet, who is more than half-Dutch. Quite a Fellini/Nino Rota atmosphere altogether. Craig Brown on a unicycle. Terence Blacker as a fire-eater. Lynn Barber as a Red Indian squaw having knives thrown at her by my old geography teacher. Documentary film-maker Tony Palmer spinning plates. Dame Beryl Bainbridge in a crushed velvet tutu tried to get up on the high wire. Francis Wheen talked politics all night with a Hungarian clown. I asked a blonde midget what it was like being shot out of a cannon. She looked up at me daggers. She wasn't actually in the circus business but was the wife of an editor off the *Sunday Express*. Paul B. was so smitten by or with Rik Hall's bum his dog whistle peeped. The night ended with the Wheel of Death and Norman's budgies. Earlier that day, Keith Floyd's funeral had been held somewhere near Bristol, and he had more famous people failing to RSVP and go to his do than even I had not coming to mine, which was a comfort of a kind.

~

Not even Stephen Fry swung by. He'd categorically told me hand-on-heart that wild horses wouldn't keep him away from my circus party – but they did. He had a meeting in Isleworth instead. "Boo hoo. So sorry." I no longer think Stephen exists as an actual flesh and blood person. He has lost weight – so much weight he has vanished, vaporised. Now he tweets, he twitters, he twats. He flits and floats in viral space merely – a hologram at best, like Olivier in the Cliff Richard musical.

~

When *Masterchef* was on with their plates of fussy food, I was busy cooking Co-op pork chops, accompanied by dry/soggy Co-op oven chips, whilst having a good old slurp of Co-op Cote du Rhone, @ £3.49. Fucking *bliss*.

~

Charlie in The Rosie announced his wife has got polyps. I asked in a tolerant way about the prognosis. "Not very good. Got the results yesterday. Twelve to eighteen months. It cost me £9 in parking."

~

I was bidden to a hush-hush meeting at the Cabinet Office – or to be precise, to a meeting with the Honours Secretariat of the Cabinet Office, in Admiralty Arch. I was under consideration for membership of the Arts and Culture Committee, which chooses the people for their medals and ribbons. I took my shopping list with me: knighthoods for Ronald Searle, Craig Brown, Richard Ingrams, Francis Wheen, Andrew Roberts, me (naturally) and Norman Barrett. Dameships for Barbara Windsor, Liz Smith, Rosie Boycott, Paul Bailey... It was all over very quickly. "What do you think about a knighthood for Brucie?" asked a man in his shirt sleeves who kept smiling like a razor, named Lord Stevenson. "In that case, it has to be Dame Cilla as well," I replied. "And Sir Ronnie Corbett."

I launched into my little prepared speech about how the Honours List must eradicate this snobbish division between those who are at the RSC or the National for five minutes and who are rewarded with automatic CBEs and knighthoods, and those in popular entertainment and television who are lucky to get an OBE, and even then it'll be "for services to charity" – I said it was a scandal that a great man like Ronnie Barker went to his grave with only an OBE, and surely a knighthood was wasted on Tom Courtenay? Smiles had by now frozen on people's faces. The bearded civil servant present had stopped taking notes. He literally let his pen fall from his fingers with a plop.

I asked what special plans might be afoot for the Queen's Diamond Jubilee in 2012 and for the Centenary of the Order of the British Empire in 2017? None obviously – because Lord Stevenson, barely containing his sarcasm, said, "You seem to know a lot about it all...You are a *student* of the Honours system, I see!" This is true. Keeps the mind alive. I wanted to ask about why we couldn't have a system more like the one in France or Italy, where the Ordre des Arts et Lettres and the Ordine al Merito della Repubblica Italiana are handed out much more generously, indeed freely. But I'd lost them again and instead the bearded civil servant chap handed me an expenses form for my travel and subsistence

— £44 Day Return from Great Malvern and £4.95 for a brie baguette from Upper Crust on Paddington Station. "By the way," said Lord Stevenson, a pal of Lord Mandelson's and like him a figure of subtlety and intrigue, "Who *is* Liz Smith?"

Michael Gove says when his lot come to power I can be put in charge of arts and culture honours — and I'll hold him to that, even though he thinks he was joking.

~

The day had got off to a bad start. A cab at the door to take me to the 7.14 train. Except it wasn't a cab. It was a man from Cake Creations delivering cakes to the sheltered accommodation opposite. I had to hop out and mutter apologies. The driver must have thought he was about to be mugged for his meringues. The real cab pulled up behind and off I went. Fuck me dead, though, this is only the third time such a mishap has occurred. Some years ago I jumped in to what wasn't a taxi but a Hillman Hunter with a man in it waiting for his wife, who was over at the doctors' surgery. More recently, my friend Stephen Moss went to Leominster in the Cake Creations van, believing it to be his minicab to Worcester Foregate Street railway station.

~

Crime Wave Corner: Six pushchairs were stolen in Clehonger, the thieves crossing a field and finding their way "through a gap in a hedge" before "making off in the direction of Kingstone, police believe." A tractor cab was stolen from a locked compound in Ross-on-Wye by what the police are again chancing their arm and calling "thieves". Meanwhile, over in Leominster, Councillor Molly Cooke "has her concerns" about a leaf that is missing from "a piece of civic furniture." Councillor Cooke told the Town Council, "It used to be kept under the stairs but I can't find it." Councillor Westwood has assured the waiting world, "We will do our best to track down the missing leaf."

~

In ghastly Clive James' new book of memoirs he says "I would have liked to have been in England when Larkin died" – perhaps the most conceited sentence in print since Anthony Burgess announced, "I was in Russia when Hemingway died." I was in Totnes when Ian Wallace croaked. What of it ?

~

I was in Totnes as Oscar is now at Dartington College of Arts, except he's home every other week to share his laundry with us. Or else his friends from The Rosie go to Devon and camp on his floor – so many of them I said why don't they simply shut the pub and tow it to Totnes and carry on boozing as usual. If they did academic courses in boozing Oscar would be its Regius Professor at All Souls.

~

But it is not my cup of tea, Dartington College of Arts. "We work together for the advancement of the arts, social justice and sustainability," it says in a leaflet. I have honestly no idea what that might conceivably mean, unless they labour long at the manufacture of floral clocks? All I noticed were lots of lady potters, ethnic beads, re-usable macramé sanitary pads, felt shoes and hats, knee-length cardigans, do-your-own-bookbinding classes, Fair Trade decaff, extensive gardens with morose old folk walking in them, and green funerals – "We also offer ethically invested pre-payment funeral plans." Puke. Oscar and the rest of the undergraduates are very sensibly decamping to a new facility at Falmouth next year.

~

Our farmhouse b & b was run by a witch called Mrs Hengist who wanted us out by 8.45 on the morrow. "I've got things to do." I wanted to about-turn the moment I saw her carpet and nasty knick-knacks and the incredibly talentless oil-effect reproductions of ships in trouble on the sea. But of course we stayed and sheepishly went along with the strictures. A lot of tut-tutting at 8.44 a.m. when I wanted to pay by credit-card, even though she had a credit-card machine there on her desk as large as fucking life. The only thing that brought a smile to Mrs Hengist's face was when she was describing the long tail-backs and traffic delays on the M5 and how a coach full of locals from Bovey Tracy heading for the Birmingham Hippodrome to see John Barrowman had missed their matinée. That made me inwardly roar too.

But in a way, how splendid that hallowed British b & b landladies from hell still exist, like Cockney cabbies talking right-wing shite, or cantankerous pub landlords, or ruddy-cheeked squires in plus-fours waving shotguns at courting couples and ramblers.

There is a friendly big black transvestite in Totnes who works in Morrisons and has changed his name officially to Hollywood Divine. Which reminds me that Tristan's circus did a Pink Night in Brighton (of course), where the comperes for the evening were called Lola Lasagne and Maisie Trollope. Maisie Trollope came in on a horse.

~

Talking of cross-dressing, was Mary Whitehouse aware that most of the sour old ladies attending her rallies were in fact immaculately attired transvestites taking the piss? "Oh we used to *live* for The Festival of Light," an elderly gent who used to go by the name of Gretel told me recently, with a real pang of nostalgia.

~

Overheard from a neighbouring table in Mahis, our Indian eatery: "Scatter cushions really *are* the way forward." I think they were talking about interior decoration, but not necessarily.

November

I'm still seething about this. A Magdalen College, Oxford, Gourmet Dinner @ £100 a head. What was I thinking of, as I don't have money to waste like that? I stay in bed because I can't afford to put the heating on. The boiler is making scary noises anyway. Like a latter-day Mimi from *La Bohème* I lie under the damp bedclothes leafing through dire celebrity memoirs by Ant and Dec, Jo Brand, Andy Williams and Val Doonican. If it wasn't for the fact that my tiny hand is frozen I'd slit my wrists. I even had to do a piece on Paul Newman the other day. Why did nobody think to ask him to play Dorian Gray, incidentally – because he surely *was* Dorian Gray and without a portrait in the attic, either? I suppose Joanne Woodward did duty for that. His salad dressing made a change from celebrity perfume.

~

Anyway this Magdalen Dinner was to be held in London, which was the first mistake. The food would just about have passed muster at a provincial wedding reception, with beans and carrots and boiled potatoes out of the freezer. The pinkish pudding was melting and had to be chased around the plate. Only one glass of wine per head, which is no good to me. It wasn't the way the Ukrainian waitresses kept dropping everything down the back of my neck that infuriated me, it was when a Guest Speaker got on his hind legs and started moaning about how Magdalen needed a few million for this, a few million for that... I did not know this was a crass fund-raising night – which I felt was disrespectful to the non-college guests present. So I got up and walked out, only wishing I'd had a few wheat germ rolls to chuck at the smug sods on Top Table. If the college is that strapped for cash – which it isn't – then they should sell up and turn it into a Travelodge. Anna and I ran away to seek solitude at the Groucho and drank Dry Martinis. We really scampered, Anna taking her shoes off and waddling barefoot up St Martin's Lane, as if we were in a Stanley Donen musical. It was like breaking free from a mausoleum. Next to us on a stool was the drummer from Blur. Or was he the blur from Drummer ?

~

The only thing to cheer me up is when I notice that those snooty little academics' sales ranking on Amazon is round about 3,000,000. Ha ha ha.

~

Because I know a lot about W.H. Auden and a lot about Benjamin Britten, and Humphrey Carpenter (biographer of both) was a personal friend, nobody has asked me to comment on Alan Bennett's new play at the National, *The Habit of Art*, which as it happens is about W.H Auden, Benjamin Britten and biographer of both, Humphrey Carpenter. I know a lot about Alan Bennett, too. We have corresponded for years. It is such a bewildering waste of my *mind*, surely? As Orson Welles used to lament, I hold all the best cards and they won't let me play poker. Instead Welles advertised frozen peas, Japanese whisky and dog food and I stay in bed reviewing the memoirs of Pauline Prescott.

~

And apropos of my non-starter of a career (I have no stipend, no annuity) – I pitched a few ideas to an editor. He wasn't keen. "Sorry about that," he said. Is there a more pusillanimous phrase in the language? Your flight is delayed. *Sorry about that.* It's inoperable. *Sorry about that.* I don't love you anymore. *Sorry about that.* I'm pregnant...

~

Actually, I do have a pension. Twenty years ago like a complete fool I was prevailed upon by a Financial Advisor arsehole to place a lump sum from a publisher's advance in the care of NatWest and hence out of my reach for ever and ever. I have now been informed that owing to the wizardry and acumen of NatWest, it is going to be worth £23.34 a month.

~

A new barmaid at The Rosie called Joy. "She never looks you in the eye," I said. "She's a trained chiropodist," I was told – and my fellow boozers are not wits. They did not write one-liners for Sid Caesar's *Your Show of Shows*. Joy also has a diploma in teeth-whitening.

~

Men as they get older start to look like women – Gareth Hunt, Ken Russell, Melvyn Bragg... No unqualified person can tell Peter O'Toole and Sian Phillips apart, even at medium close-up range. When Michael Winner tottered towards me I thought it was a reincarnation of my grandmother, Martha Evelyn George from Haverfordwest, who after a mild stroke was bundled off into the glue factory at Ystrad Mynach, where she lingered for over a decade, getting hairier and crankier. Grandma George grew cactuses in her bay window, as coincidentally enough I now grow cactuses in mine. It must be genetic. Cactuses are imposing, ugly, aggressive, abnormally shaped, and once in a blue moon they'll bear a solitary brilliantly coloured flower.

Forty years after the war was over, Grandma George was

still complaining about the evacuees who were billeted in her huge and gloomy farmhouse in Upper Machen called The Gelli, which is no doubt Welsh for Wuthering Heights. My parents sent me to live with her at The Gelli when I was eight, an experience of loneliness and warmed-up gravy dinners I against expectations thoroughly enjoyed. It started a theme with which I was to become familiar – being at home yet not at home everywhere I go or try and settle.

Michael Winner kindly said I could bring along who I liked to his do at the Belvedere – so I thought it might be funny to take him at his word and stroll in accompanied by the Herefordshire Police Male Voice Choir. Instead I took the Hungarian clowns from Zippo's Circus.

~

Patrick Garland told me a good story about circus tumblers. Why, it was asked by a younger comedian during the days of music hall and variety, did the comedians top the bill? And, for all their brilliance and facility, why were the acrobats, knife-throwers, and so on, always far lower down? "They're lower down the bill than us, son," said an old stand-up to his apprentice, "because they are too lazy to learn a fucking comic song." I find that this is a lesson – a rubric – applicable to many, many situations to be met with throughout life. It has a moral meaning or dimension and should be carved in marble and set above lintels. *Don't Be Too Fucking Lazy To Learn A Comic Song*. It should be translated into Latin.

~

These tangerine-coloured celebrities look dog-rough up

close. Joanna Lumley looked as if she'd fallen face first in her mascara jar. Perhaps she tripped over a lurking Ghurkha. Ann Robinson can no longer blink. One more facelift and she can go out and about pretending to be Acker Bilk. Indeed, there was enough Botox in that room to freeze the waters of the moon.

~

John McEntee introduced me to Michael Caine and his wife Shakira, the pop singer. I told Sir Caine that should they make a film of my life – with Simon Russell Beale in Chekhov mode as me: there is a vague possibility that this might happen – would he play my father, South Welsh gentleman-farmer and virtually bankrupt-butcher, Matthias Llywelyn Dafydd Owain Madog Ap Gruffudd Lewis? "It would not be a taxing part," I assured Sir Caine, who in a flash was doing what normally only amateur dramatic actors or National Theatre artistes do to express horror, surprise and consternation – i.e., holding up his hands, palms outwards, and taking a full pace backwards, tilting slightly from the vertical as he did so. It is not true, though, as was reported in some newspapers, that he also tried to run out of the room. "My father was either asleep or dead," I explained, keeping my nerve.

~

Regarding underplaying – how the golly heck did Alec Guinness get a reputation for minimalist acting as George Smiley in *Tinker, Tailor, Soldier, Spy*? The usual view is that he's hardly doing anything – those blank, inscrutable stares. But if you watch his performance today – his vigorous half-smiles, moues, frowns, blinks, gazes, twitches, tics, glasses on, glasses off: it is sheer Grand Guignol, his face and pursed lips going like the clappers, like Klaus Kinski with ants in his pants doing a kabuki routine, with the camera over-cranked for humorous effect. Guinness is also rather camp, in a creepy rather than a joyous way.

~

I've just re-read the Smiley books (and watched for the sixth time Alec Guinness in the DVDs) and what I noticed is how absolutely antiquated it all is – the manila folders, the dog-eared paperwork, the creeping about in Pall Mall gentlemen's clubs. No computers. No CCTVs. No electronic surveillance. People smoking. People *drinking*!

They could be in the Age of Elizabeth I, eavesdropping from behind curtains, having secret confabs on Hampstead Heath. And, of course, underneath it all – the codes and practices of the public school. Nobody is nasty to Bill Haydon when he is unmasked – he is killed by an ex-lover (the underrated Ian Bannen) over some lingering tiff. Nothing to do with his political/patriotic betrayals. It would have been bad form to have brought any of that up, like mentioning to Old Etonian Captain Hook that he had a false arm. Ian Richardson told me that that bit at the end where Haydon pockets Smiley's fountain pen – he (Ian) wanted to put that in, to suggest a slimy nature. Otherwise there was nothing in the script to make us not like him.

All gone, now, Smiley's world, yet it was only the

seventies. For a remake, those offices and streets would have to be painstakingly reconstructed by art directors and set decorators and shot on specially prepared grimy film-stock. The books aren't prescient – unless the theme of power and paranoia at the heart of Whitehall is seen as endemic. There are plenty of contemporary politicians who'd not have been out of place in Le Carré's versions of a Renaissance court, but they'd have to start smoking and drinking.

What didn't seem to come off – Smiley's romantic agony about Lady Anne (played by Mrs Peter O'Toole – Sian Phillips). I don't think that extra (adulterous) undercurrent totally worked (or was necessary). Karla, too, has these thwarted feelings for his daughter, who is locked up in a clinic. It all stops being about espionage and cross and double-cross and becomes about lonely ogres pining for love in their castles. Like *Beauty and the Beast* or *The Phantom of the Opera*. Le Carré tries to turn it all into a fairy story.

The much earlier *The Spy Who Came in from the Cold* is a great book – the stuff about espionage/acting/dissembling/losing a grip on reality could be about the psychology of Peter Sellers.

~

Hoisting herself on the scales, a member of my Slimming World class said, "I weigh more tonight because it's so cold I've got my big knickers on." Oh God Strike Me Pink! One day I am going to collapse and never regain consciousness.

~

The Things You See When You Haven't Got A Gun (2):

Boris's back-combed sister Rachel came running out of the hairdressers and chased me along Holland Park Avenue. "Get back, lady, unless you like the taste of mace!" I was ready to say. "Are you mad Roger from Hertfordshire?" she asked in a non-hostile way. Indeed, her manner was almost hearty. "There's more than one category mistake in that sentence," I ventured, ripe for a philosophy debate right there and then.

But I don't think Rachel wanted to go into that side of it. Instead she asked me to write about Joanna Lumley for *The Lady* – a publication Rachel with aplomb thinks she has been summoned by the wisdom of Almighty God to make cool and camp and trendy (some hope).

Rachel says her office hasn't been decorated since the Coronation. So what? So *what*? My house hasn't been painted since Queen Victoria's Diamond Jubilee. The roof is sliding off, the glass is falling out of the windows, the garden is one big drooping mass of weeds, the children stay in bed all day hung-over on Weston's cider, and I haven't had full sex since Anna had her ovaries whipped out.

Anyway, I tell Gyles that Rachel Johnson wants me to write about Joanna Lumley for *The Lady* and that I think Joanna Lumley is annoyingly over-praised, that *Ab Fab* was total mirthless shite, and that I hope that these 30,000 Nepalese families who are going to come over here and claim benefits *all camp out in Joanna Lumley's fucking front garden*. She'll be cutting sandwiches for the rest of her life.

Gyles said Joanna Lumley was his best friend and "she

was in the best production of *The Cherry Orchard* I've ever seen." I said, who'd she play? Old Firs?

~

Duncan Fallowell came in with a plate of mince pies, "Christmas has *begun*!" He had been house-hunting in the Herefordshire Balkans, intending to switch his villa in St Tropez for a cottage in Hope-under-Dinmore. As usual he'd had his assignations in cowsheds with ploughboys. The people he meets. Lorry drivers leap from their cabs and pursue him up the stairs, Biggles-style pilots at Shobdon airdrome reveal to him that up in their De Havilland DH-60 biplanes they are wearing bra and panties and Fanny Cradock ball gowns. Duncan is turning the Herefordshire Balkans into Pagan Greece.

~

If Duncan decamps to Hope-under-Dinmore the total number of authors in the Herefordshire Balkans will rise to four, as currently there's only Roy Strong, Quentin Letts, and me. Or, as Sad Mother Julie Myerson, 48, would have it, three – as currently there's only Roy Strong and Quentin Letts.

~

Crime Wave Corner: it's getting to be as bad as Helmand Province here. There have been twenty-two burglaries from sheds this year – mowers, strimmers and bicycles "have all been taken in the raids". A steam cleaner and a litre of red diesel have gone missing from Alton Road. Firefighters "were called to a blaze in a tumble dryer" in Glewstone, and then the same (or a similar) crew had to "release a dog from a Morris Traveller". Mercifully, "there were no reports that the animal was harmed" – then or later. What I want to know is how an eleven-month-old Corgi had locked itself in and turned on the ignition in the first place, as "the engine was still running."

~

You know when The Mark of Death is upon an old lady in Bromyard. They start going out and about with their tartan trolleys, wearing a St Michael's Hospice chemotherapy wig. There's only one style – a startling blonde bob. The Mark of Death is upon them and they look like Dora Bryan.

~

The Groucho's Gourmet Dinner, cooked by Stéphane Reynaud, was a most superior event and, compared with Magdalen's rip-off, @ £55 a head a total bargain. My guest this time was Young Antony from The Rosie. He arrived late without explanation and already well-refreshed. His phone kept going off – Jason had been left behind in a managerial capacity for the first time and wanted to know, "Can I move the beer that's in the shed?" Lisa phoned up and said, "What are you going to buy me in the Burlington Arcade?" I felt like going outside into Dean Street and calling Young Antony up and saying, "Will you turn your fucking phone off?" Young Antony stayed at the Dorchester, ending his night talking in the bar with a high-class hooker, though he didn't know that's what she was at the time. He thought she was Nicole Kidman. He asked me a day or so later, "Do they have hookers at the Travelodge?" – my budget accommodation of choice, so sod off. "Yes – but they've got spots," I said.

~

The Travelodge had checked me into a disabled room, by the way – a shower you could get your wheelchair in and out of, plus space for the carer, and chrome bars around the toilet, so you could do pull-ups if you felt like it, as at the gym.

~

Photographs of Lady Antonia Fraser always make me laugh so dementedly I do number ones – Lady Antonia grinning inanely as she takes a chisel to the Berlin Wall; Lady Antonia simpering at Salman Rushdie and Václav Havel; Lady Antonia sitting astride a tombstone outside East Coker church, Somerset, in the mistaken belief she is visiting that other T.S. Eliot place of pilgrimage, Little Gidding, which is near Cambridge.

For Lady Antonia Fraser resembles Dame Edna Everage. The tapering height, the big hair, the fluffy opal clothes, the costume jewellery: Lady Antonia must get fed up with oiks yelling *Hello, Possums!* to her in the street.

But the remarkable likeness between the bow-legged Melbourne megastar and "the Catholic aristocrat with her title"* doesn't end with the physical stunt-doubling. Lady Antonia has acquired Dame Edna's New Age philosophy.

---

* Which is what top-drawer moll Lady Antonia helpfully calls herself in *Must You Go? My Life With Harold Pinter* (Weidenfeld & Nicolson) – *the* most rib-tickling book in blinking years.

"Be calm, have a calm centre, turn towards the calm centre and inspect it, contemplate my soul," intones Lady Antonia in a far-away manner – a manner that reminded me of Dame Edna's admonition that "I share and I care."

The caring, of course, can come to an abrupt halt. Just as Dame Edna on her chat show would remove boring guests by pushing a lever to open a trapdoor, so Lady Antonia finds that tolerance and compassion can only extend *so far*. When Pat Naipaul complains about Sir Vidia's anger and violence, Lady Antonia laments that she's "not quite strong enough for lame ducks at present." Then in the next breath she mews quietly and sighs, "I felt the most terrible guilt for everything in the world," and not only that, "when my basset hound died in 1985, I didn't believe that animals had souls. But now I do." I don't think even Dame Edna thought she was Jesus and St Francis of Assisi rolled into one.

And then there is Harold Pinter, her very own Norm. If Norm, famously the first patient in medical history to survive a prostate transplant, had returned from Gallipoli with a metal plate in his head, then that is Lady Antonia's conception of her man Pinter – a hero whose "force is burning me up and fascinating me all at the same time."

The rest of us might form the opinion that Harold was more of a certifiable lunatic in need of a tranquillising dart. "He attacked the attendant for opening the door in the middle of the recital," we are told of one typical night out. On another occasion he was nasty to the Nicaraguan Minister of Culture, "under the impression she was Bianca Jagger."

I'd have welcomed more information on how his "continual obsession with spies" manifested itself. Did Harold compulsively look under beds and in wardrobes? Did he conceal himself behind the furniture and pounce with ferocity on complete strangers if they wore carnations in their buttonholes? His growling, taciturn vocal delivery might be explained by his fear that his conversation was being bugged, and that he was under surveillance by waiters and taxi drivers, probably even muffin men and sweeps.

Harold took Lady Antonia home after a dinner party and "stayed until six o'clock in the morning with extraordinary recklessness." Perhaps he'd locked himself in the toilet and had to wait until he was set free by one of the multicultural domestic staff, up at dawn to light the fires.

Harold, we are told, lived in "an enormous stately six-storey house in Regents Park Terrace", crammed with an extensive art collection. Did Lady Antonia not realise when she went for tea in February 1975 that she was visiting the wrong house? Harold lived in Hanover Terrace, not Regents Park Terrace.

We don't hear about the final fate of Harold's salubrious pad, perhaps because Lady Antonia's descriptions of the "extremely sumptuous" residence belonged to a total stranger, and whoever it was who emerged from the shadows to say "I'll show you my study presently" might well have been someone else entirely – Sir Les Patterson perhaps; or Kingsley Amis – who lived nearby at 194 Regents Park Road, Primrose Hill. But now things are starting to get too confusing.

Harold's predecessor more or less in Lady Antonia's affections was thirsty mummer Robert Stephens. Stephens was some distance into his affair with Lady Antonia before it was pointed out to him by the medically qualified wife of Jonathan Miller that he was in the midst of a severe nervous breakdown. He went into the mental home adjacent to the Hospital of Tropical Diseases in Camden for ten weeks.

He must have had at least one afternoon at large again, because my friend Paul saw him from the top of a bus wandering around Campden Hill Square in floods of tears. Lady Antonia brings up none of this in her memoirs.

~

Crimewave Corner: Officers in Leominster are appealing for witnesses after a truly appalling incident. A man "dressed in black" threw a stone at the local church, "which left a dent in the door". Bearded churchwarden David Russell was pictured in the local paper pointing abjectly at the small scratch. Nevertheless, anyone with further information is to call Crimestoppers on 0800 555 111.

~

I took myself to luncheon in Rules, Maiden Lane. A pair of silly old fools in the upstairs bar, the wife reading the menu out loud to her husband – every single blasted item, from potted shrimps to sherry trifle. Was he blind? Illiterate? A certified imbecile likely to soil himself? Or simply too lazy to learn a comic song?

"Spinach. You don't like spinach do you?" – "You can always leave it off. I'll eat it, but I don't want it." They decided on some big rib of beef dish. "You've got to have that for two. I can't have it if you don't want it. Go through it again..." Chase my Aunt Fanny round a mulberry bush, but the lady read the whole menu out loud once more at dictation speed, from potted shrimps to sherry trifle.

The barman came over, which put them in a flap. "We don't serve *coffee*, or *beer*," the barman sneered – so nastily and unnecessarily I wanted to hit him. They settled on glasses of tonic water. The old couple had come to town to meet their son, whose idea luncheon at Rules evidently was. They'd already had quite enough of an adventure getting a taxi to the restaurant from the station – being convinced, as my parents always were, that the driver was deliberately taking them on a long route around the houses so as to fleece the country bumpkins. I was called to my table so I didn't clock the son, or witness what I'm convinced would be their awkward conversation – the son the first in his family to get a degree and to have a job in London, and who is now a sort of stranger to his mum and dad, who sacrificed everything to give him the chance in life they'd not had themselves. Or so I was surmising. I could be wrong. They might have had a riotous afternoon, with lots of laughs.

I lost my own battle with the barman. I asked for a drop of Amontillado in my Bloody Mary. "We don't do that *here*," he said. I hope he gets cancer of the penis.

~

My cure for global warming: air conditioning.

~

What university, I wonder, gave Professor Moriarty his Chair? The Sherlockologists would know. Might it have been the University of Central England, now Birmingham City University, and soon no doubt to be reborn and re-branded for a thousandth time as the University of Middle Earth? They ought to open The Roger Lewis Wing in any event, as I have given them millions of surplus-to-requirements books over the years, from Alastair Campbell's diaries to Alastair Campbell's novels and the memoirs of Bill Oddie.

~

To St Albans Abbey for my Graduation Ceremony from the University of Hertfordshire, to whom I have paradoxically *never* donated the works of Alastair Campbell or Bill Oddie. St Albans has all the charm of Stourport-on-Severn, where the great Ann George (Amy Turtle) kept a static caravan. St Albans has, I noticed, the grave of Robert Runcie, which is not quite of comparable interest.

~

It was like the plot of *Wild Strawberries* – a long trip by an old professor in a car to collect a doctorate. Why am I so moved – moved to tears – by *Wild Strawberries*? I literally can't talk to Anna about it without blubbing. Ridiculous. I mean it is not Ryan O'Neal and Ali McGraw in *Love Story*, is it? Or sentimental *ET* with its pounding score? I tried to describe the ending of *Wild Strawberries* when I was in Mahis and the waiters thought I'd swallowed a chilli. I was surrounded by concerned Indians who diligently commute every evening from Wolverhampton. Maybe, to the glee of my enemies, I am cracking up.

It is about emotional freezing and thawing, *Wild Strawberries*. The bit where Professor Isak Borg waves across the lake to these white-clad figures, who turn out to be apparitions of his parents in their younger days, is so tender, so beautiful. The scene is about the foreclosure of time – a dying man having a vision of the distant past. But there is vastly more to it than this, or at least there is to me.

For you see – it is a scene about love. The professor is seeing his parents when they are courting, when they were first in love, before he was born. And without that love of theirs, he himself would never have existed. None of this is spelt out, but it is there in the actor Victor Sjostrom's eyes, in his gaze.

Ingmar Bergman himself was entranced and often wrote about filming the low-angle close up – and Bergman could be a frosty fuck, difficult to impress or move. This from his diary: "We have shot... the final close-ups of Isak Borg as he is brought to clarity and reconciliation. His face shone with secretive light, as if reflected from another reality. His features become suddenly mild. His look was open, smiling... It was like a miracle. Then complete stillness – peace and clarity of soul. Never before or since have I experienced a face so noble and liberated. Yet it was all nothing more than a piece of acting in a dirty studio." Acting it had to be. Apparently Victor Sjostrom was a querulous and senile old bugger in real life. He died soon after.

~

I looked like a total twat-shaped twat in my doctoral robes, hired for the day @ £41. Except I only went and bought the costume afterwards – and now threaten to wear it round the house. A scarlet gown with purple silk stripes, a red and grey hood, and a silly velvet bonnet with a tassel. Oscar said I looked like a member of the defunct Bromyard Ladies Singers. Defunct because the vicar brought in bongos – also, out went "Dearly Beloved" and in came "Hi, I'm Graham."

~

"Right," I screamed. "Who's the filthy beast?" I dangled for all to see a scanty thong I'd fished out of the washing machine. "It's *disgusting*! That's what this is, *disgusting*!" My suspicions fell on Vicky Christina Budapesta, who has apple-green eye shadow to match her apple-green thigh-length boots, and who is currently bumping Tristan bandy. She has so many piercings and holes drilled about her face for studs and chains, should she sneeze it would be like the Trevi Fountain. The season over, Tristan's circus caravan is outside by the back gate – which annoys the neighbours, who wouldn't object I am sure to a yacht or a polo pony horsebox. Anyway it was not a thong after all, but the muslin cover from a Fortnum's Christmas Pudding.

~

The local press here said that I had been given a doctorate by the University of Herefordshire, which doesn't exist. You'd have thought *The Hereford Times* and *The Western Mail* would know this. To get them to print a rectification will be to enter a parallel cosmos of intensifying humiliation, like when Mr Pooter tries to get them to correct his name from Mr Porter in the guest list at the Mansion House Ball. All our post is always erroneously addressed to Hertfordshire, anyway. I demand a reduction in my rates.

~

What is it Strindberg used to say? That he suffered most from the pain "of not being what I most would be." As the year ends, news reaches me from the Royal Society of Literature that, as I have been turned down for a Fellowship *a record number of times*, the Committee does not want to hear my name spoken of again until at least three or thirty further years have elapsed. So there we are: I am officially the least recognised and most non-esteemed author in Britain, perhaps in Britain's literary history going back to Chaucer and beyond Chaucer to *The Mabinogion* – as welcome to the Establishment as a toxic spillage.

"I'm truly astonished," gasped my friend Jan Morris, when she saw me crying my eyes out, "that being the person you are, you give a tinker's cuss for the Royal Society of Literature! Dear God, isn't being Roger Lewis *enough* for you? There are dozens and dozens of FRSLs, but only one of *him*!" It is funny how the people who try to console me so very sweetly have themselves been Fellows of the Royal Society of Literature for donkey's years – Jan herself, Cousin Jeremy, Paul Bailey, Lynne Truss, Kathryn Hughes, Philip Hensher, hundreds of others. Get a petition going, guys! I want to be the equivalent of Deirdre as The Weatherfield One.

I'm from a South Welsh swamp. I've had enough of being *curbed* and *stunted* and *spurned*. This is why I seethe. Why I grow paranoid. Were I a Shakespearean king there'd be executions. There'd be *broils*.

Being Roger Lewis of course isn't enough – it isn't even nearly more than enough. It is nothing. There are two others that I know of who are something, by the way. There's a Roger Lewis in New York who runs a shoe factory. And there's an august one in Wales who runs the Welsh Rugby Union and who used to be the chairman of Classic FM. He wrote to me once. He was fed up of *Goon Show* fans clobbering him for saying Peter Sellers was off his head in more than a manner of speaking. I said people are cross with me for the rubbish broadcast on Classic FM.

No doubt if I were elected President of the British Academy, awarded the OM, and if Billie Piper insisted on giving me that blow job, all within the same hour, I'd find fault. The only thing to give me pleasure these days – and which turns me away from my desolation and psychopathic dreaming, like Frankenstein's monster switching his expression to a sorrowful smile when he hears the violin music and tries to catch the notes with his big hands as they float by him on the breeze – are Matisse's cut-outs. The sculptures of pure colour, of under-the-sea shapes and blooms, of dancers and acrobats.

**Tristan juggling – a skill not taught at
Magdalen College, Oxford**

Oscar

Sébastien

APPENDIX

Doctor Lewis sees the first ten years of the New Millennium as characterised by a tilt towards paranoia, mistrust, stupidity and politically correct timidity. You can't even put sugar in your tea now ...

If my grandfather Cyril Absolom Brynley George came back from the dead, he'd insist on rendering himself up again to the sulphurous flames at top speed. These days we can't smoke, we are frowned upon if we drink, and we can't hunt foxes – and my grandfather, an MFH in Glamorganshire, did all three simultaneously. He also enjoyed ogling women with big boobs and took too much sugar in his tea. We can't do that anymore, either.

Just as *Carry On* babe Barbara Windsor turned from an arse-wiggler with Sid James into the drudge and scold of Albert Square, so it was in the noughties that naughtiness came to an end – to be replaced with a pervasive priggishness. We can't have Christmas carols in shops or canteens, in case people of other faiths are offended. I find this a bizarre ruling in the Herefordshire Balkans, where I hang my hat. The only practitioners of other faiths you'll find are folklorists and the odd hairy wizard.

Nevertheless, if like supply teacher Olive Jones or nurse Caroline Petrie you offer to remember your pupils or patients in your prayers, you risk the sack. The only characters permitted to voice strong feelings and express fervent beliefs are the Muslims. Gentle Jesus, meek and mild, has had the chop, particularly now that the C of E's nancy vicars are to be sent by the Archbishop of Canterbury to Kampala for execution.

It has become a charged word, however, faith. One of my resentments about the MPs and their greed and hubris over their lavish expenses, was that they excused their larceny as accidents and mistakes "made in good faith". The mortgage fiddles, the hanging baskets, the bathplugs and entire second homes... Similarly, the Iraq War, which was waged on false claims about non-existent big bombs, was another instance of errors and fudging being given credence "in good faith" – Blair's exact words. Holy Wars involving terrorists and martyrs and men in turbans takes us right back to the Crusades of the Middle Ages. Blair thought of himself as a dashing Errol Flynn. In fact he was Claude Rains's oily Prince John, with Mandelson his saturnine Sheriff of Nottingham.

We don't trust the politicians, they don't trust us – they don't even trust themselves. Remember the arrest of Damian Green and the ransacking of his office at the Palace of Westminster, when police removed files and laptops? It was like East Germany under Honecker. No wonder Harriet Harman now wears a stab vest.

Honesty and integrity are other things that have vanished into the past. Money, for example, was treated by our economic masters as an abstraction, a mirage – until, during the financial sector's recent *dance macabre*, jobs were lost, bills couldn't be paid, and houses repossessed. Meanwhile, the rapacious bankers and the hedge fund managers, who orchestrated the calamities, have not been seen to suffer personally. Indeed, having received billions from the taxpayer, they still receive whopping bonuses, despite national insolvency and stock prices falling to zero. I'd erect a guillotine, if put in charge.

To be suspicious of everyone, to doubt their motives, is now endemic. Pat a child on the head, smile at infants enjoying themselves on a swing, and you'll be branded a paedo. We soon won't be allowed to change our own children's nappies, unless we stand behind a glass screen and wear industrial-strength rubber gloves. There'll be CCTV cameras in every home and certainly in every classroom. For we already live in an atmosphere of surveillance, with microchips to monitor the greenness of our garbage. Our number plates are automatically recognised – so GCHQ know where we are going and even the South Welsh pastime of fly-tipping has had to come to an end. Emails and mobile phone calls are also stored by the authorities, the Top Secret computer files and disks routinely left on trains and in taxis so we can all have a gander.

Whether we want to commit a serious crime, a terrorist atrocity, or simply hope to send our children to a school in a neighbouring catchment area, the same draconian laws are deployed. The government doesn't want us to be free souls, and under the guise of promising to protect us is actually seeking to regulate human nature. Our libel courts have stamped out both freedom of speech and the voicing of strong opinions. Alexei Sayle was sued when he made a joke. It is now better to let patients die than incur the wrath of a pharmaceutical firm's legal team, if it is suggested that their drugs could do with a bit of testing.

Mad litigation of all kinds is prevalent. As up to 3.6 million people in Britain are allergic to latex, it is "best to avoid balloons" at office parties, and also mistletoe must no longer deck the room as it "might encourage flirtatious remarks which could be construed as sexual harassment," according to county council guidelines I saw the other day. The upshot of the paranoia is that people are retreating from real flesh and blood encounters. Instead they log on to their computers. They twitter, they tweet, they twat. Relationships take place on Facebook and they watch each other on YouTube.

People believe themselves to be connected to the world, but actually they are quite separated from it, gazing at a screen, where life is crushed and withered, not physical but viral or virtual. People think they've gone global, yet they are still in the back bedroom. Next to my clocking Stephen Fry poking his Blackberry in Trafalgar Square during the Two Minute Silence, the oddest thing I ever witnessed concerning the Internet was when I went up the River Amazon. There we were in the jungle and a woman from Diss was doing her on-line Tesco's shopping.

But of course I couldn't mock, let alone throw her overboard to be eaten by piranhas. We are not allowed to pass judgement about people now. Harriet Harman is seeing to this. Harriet is Minister for Women and Equality! – the anti-male, anti-talent bias of that makes the blood fairly drain from the corpus collosum. It is going to be officially no longer permitted to look up to anyone – doctors, teachers, priests, artists. Everyone is going to be as dowdy as a social worker – as dowdy as little Hattie Harman herself.

The proposed legislation about equality means that the stupider and more amateurish you are, the better. If you are bald, gay, walk with a limp and are from an ethnic minority as well, you're laughing. You'll be a People's Peer. This is both the extension and consequence of Reality TV, where mediocrity has replaced substance and graft, where expertise and knowledge are dirty words – the equivalent of being elitist or snobbish. Lord Mandelson's call for fast-track degrees and his announcement that £135 million is to be lopped from the Higher Education budget will help this trend along nicely.

In the arts, with CGI and cartoons, there is now no need for actual acting or drawing skills. And just as nobody writes letters – people prefer the trivia of texting – nobody reads books, which are going the way of steam trains and sailing ships and horse-drawn ploughs. Indeed, the only books bookshops want to sell and publishers publish are the ghosted memoirs of television celebrities, where chapter after chapter concerns their cellulite.

Reality? Locking people in an over-lit house or sending them into a rain forest to suffer endless humiliations always looked mightily contrived to me. The contestants, as also with these warblers and egotists on talent shows, are manipulated into crying and showing off and the television companies must be getting a group discount at The Priory. Simon Cowell, a man who perhaps represents the spirit of our age like no other, is in fact a reincarnation of Hughie Greene – not a nice thing to be.

Who wants real or ordinary people anyway? I want Dame Judi Dench in a bonnet. But the most iconic female figure of the New Millennium is not an accomplished person – indeed, she was defiantly the reverse of accomplished. Step forward Saint Jade Goody, whose Eau de Parfum Spray does brisk business on eBay. Jade, who though vilified at first, obligingly died young of cancer and instantly became a goddess. "Look," she told Max Clifford, "I'm thick as two short planks. I open my mouth and put my foot in it."

For Jade – and for the millions who have called for her canonisation – her ignorance was blissful, her blandness and brashness a sign of unadorned innocence. The authoress of *Jade: How It All Began, Jade: Fighting To The End, Jade: Catch A Falling Star, Jade: Forever In My Heart,* and *Jade: Remember Me This Way*, she is what passed for being natural, like one of those noble savages in eighteenth-century philosophy.

It is just that well-educated people with nice manners, like me for example, feel left out of things more than ever.

When an edited version of the above appeared in the Daily Telegraph, *readers shook Roger Lewis's hand in the street.*

ACKNOWLEDGEMENTS

Since I started sending my splenetic antidote to Christmas round-robins out to my friends a few years ago, they have been urging me to seek publication. I am pleased to say that my editor Aurea Carpenter saw at once what I was up to and this project got itself off the ground with surprisingly little ado. We had a nightmare with the lawyers, but that's another story. As ever, my agent and champion, Dr. Leslie Gardner, and her team at Artellus, masterminded the business arrangements – without Leslie I might still be delivering meat in South Wales from the back of a van. I hope you will now enjoy my diaries yourselves, and see how they have been evolving.

I remain eternally grateful to loyal comrades-in-arms such as Paul Bailey, Lynn Barber, Terence Blacker, Colonel Craig Brown, Barry Cryer, David H. Harries, Michael Herbert, Philip Kemp, Herbert Kretzmer, Sam Leith, Cousin Jeremy Lewis, the late Hugh Massingberd, Jonathan Meades, Mavis Nicholson, George Nestor, Tony Palmer, Sir Tim Rice, Byron Rogers, and Sergeant Frances Welch, who didn't mind in the least my going on about how the wolves are snapping at my heels, so long as I made them laugh. In fact, they egged me on in every way. I also salute Eric Bailey and George Thwaites of *The Mail on Sunday*, Catherine Jones of *The Western Mail* and Guy Adams of *The Independent* for enigmatic encouragement.

Perhaps in the end that is the only alchemy that can be relied upon, to turn tragedy (or the mundane) into comedy. But what other people have deemed my jeremiads and rants, I myself see simply and sweetly as an attempt to foster "an unsleeping sense of the ridiculous and a continual awareness of life's small poignancies and the need for courage in meeting them," as Philip Larkin said of Barbara Pym. But why bother with a peashooter if you prefer a howitzer's big bang ?

David Howard, Rik Hall, and the cast and crew of the ill-fated *Flick*, are to be thanked for providing me with years (as it turned out) of amusement. I am additonally beholden to the filmmakers for supplying their still of Faye Dunaway, Margaret John and Mark Benton. Regarding the other illustrations: the author and his father, the French magazine cover for *Moi, Peter Sellers*, and the clipping about The Whiz come from my own collection; Joe McGrath, Peter Lydon and the author were snapped by the organisers of The Cardiff Screen Festival (Gwyl Sgrîn Caerdydd) in 2004 – to whom many thanks; the splendid portrait of Nurse Thomas is from *Machen Revisited*, compiled by Delphine Coleman and Dennis Spargo (Tempus Publishing, 2001); and Mark Kehoe's portrait of Tristan juggling is used by permission of Martin Townsend, editor of *The Sunday Express*. The picture of the author and television's Maureen Lipman in Brazil was taken by Anna, and appeared in *The Mail on Sunday* in 2007.

My debts to the citizens of Herefordshire and to Anna, Tristan, Oscar and Sébastien are incapable of repayment. I must also thank Hope Pickles and her family and their dog Branston for allowing themselves to become characters in my psychodrama. Other names here and there have been changed and locations slightly disguised – because Anna said feelings might get hurt. This hadn't occurred to me. I also ought to add here that regarding the Welsh lot, they would perhaps tell some of the stories very differently – so I crave their indulgence. Anyway, as Max Beerbohm said of his caricatures, "Oh well, you know, when you exaggerate as much as that, there can be no offence in it."

I am pleased to dedicate the book – which when my hard-drive blew up was rescued by an emergency grant from The Francis Head Bequest at the Society of Authors – to a quartet of wonderful and loyal old friends, Gyles Brandreth, Duncan Fallowell, Stephen J. Masty and Francis Wheen, without whom I really would long since have cheerfully slit my throat.

Roger Lewis MA, PhD, DLitt (Hon.), FRSA, FRGS, FRAS,
Dignitas Clinic,
Postfach 9,
CH-8127 Forch,
Zurich,
Switzerland

Roger Lewis is the author of books about Laurence Olivier, Charles Hawtrey and Anthony Burgess. His international bestselling biography *The Life and Death of Peter Sellers* was adapted into a multi-award-winning film. Married to an educational psychologist and with three sons, Lewis divides his time between Herefordshire and Austria.